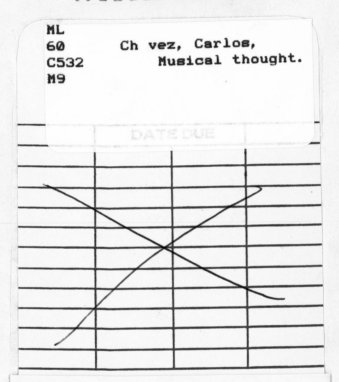

DATE DUE

Musical Thought

THE CHARLES ELIOT NORTON LECTURES

1958-1959

MUSICAL THOUGHT

Carlos Chávez

HARVARD UNIVERSITY PRESS

Cambridge, Massachusetts

1961

The musical illustrations on pages 66–67 from Gershwin's "It Ain't Necessarily So" (Copyright © 1935 by Gershwin Publishing Corporation, New York, N. Y.) are quoted by permission.

The musical illustrations on pages 70–76 from Stravinsky's Petrouchka (Copyright by Edition Russe de Musique; Copyright assigned to Boosey & Hawkes Ltd.; Revised version copyright 1947, 1948, by Boosey & Hawkes), Le Sacre du Printemps (Copyright 1921 by Edition Russe de Musique; Copyright assigned to Boosey & Hawkes Ltd.), and Threni (Copyright 1958 by Boosey & Co. Ltd.) are quoted by permission.

Contents

Musical Thought

I

A Latin American Composer

When I first heard from Archibald MacLeish, inquiring about my disposition and availability to fill the Charles Eliot Norton Chair of Poetry at Harvard University, I was flattered and puzzled. Obviously flattered, because such an invitation implies honor and recognition to anybody, and definitely puzzled because I did not know whether I would really be able to put a general summing up of my ideas in order and compose it in a presentable way. I was, on the other hand, frankly reluctant to say no without considering the matter calmly, for I would have seemed a defeatist.

So the point was to examine such a completely unexpected proposition and see how I could go about it. If the mail had brought me a letter with a commission to write

1

music, my only concern would have been time and adjustments of schedule. But the proposition, as it came, brought up new problems which were quite detached from my mind, at least at that moment. It is true that one is always thinking about general problems concerning his profession, and constantly trying to find explicable motives for what one does. However, one does not, without good reason, feel inclined to give any special effort to formulating one's own ideas in writing, particularly when the struggle against time is such that there is always barely enough to write one's own music.

Therefore there were many problems to consider, but there were also incentives, mainly two: first, the rather exploratory curiosity to give shape to themes of my predilection; and in this connection I cannot thank enough the President and Fellows of Harvard College and the Committee of the Charles Eliot Norton Professorship, who made it possible for me to sit down for a while and concentrate in order to put together scattered and wandering thoughts. Second, there was the avowed hope of getting at least a minimum of interest from an illustrious audience, such as the one I had the honor to address.

However, everything is a matter of good rapport. I shall try to tell you my story. By that I don't mean that I shall be telling you anything really personal or new. It will simply be my own way of saying it, with a certain local color. We often find much ill feeling toward local color and many things have been said against it; yet, after all, everything is a matter of local color—our face, our speech, our tastes; even cosmopolitanism is subject to it, since it is nothing but the summing up of many local colors.

The Charles Eliot Norton chair, I would say, is like a big window. Visiting professors come periodically from far and near and somehow with their person they bring to you their own milieu, thereby providing you with an opening out of which you can look. Now you have the sane curiosity to take the time to look out of this window, and I bring my own little story, all good feeling, and sincerity.

A composer or a writer—in fact, any artist—is nothing but a messenger. What we owe to ourselves is infinitesimal as compared with what we owe to others: past, present, back home, anywhere. Men, in the very early days when they began to build, built nothing but walls, solid walls, enclosures for protection and defense; and as time went by, holes were opened in walls, openings through which to see and to be seen, to hear and to be heard, by whatever forms of communication were accessible to mankind. So that nowadays, in order to defend and protect ourselves, we open windows instead of shutting them. (We distrust closed areas with much reason.) Whatever truth and happiness there may be come from communication, from opening windows. We all devoutly believe in communication; in one way or another, everybody wants to say something and wants to be heard. Man is a gregarious animal, sociologists tell us, and his gregarious sense wants no fetters or boundaries; to him all kinds of fences and curtains are inhuman, even antihuman. *PERSON WALLS FENCES*

This is where the idea of communication meets with the idea of freedom. I said "meets," but in fact they are inseparable, if each is to be effective and genuine. We want them so: and we cannot insist upon this point enough; for art, our main design, is nothing but one of the many forms of the ever-present urge for free communication.

A number of specific means of expression and understanding, which are called languages, have been developed. Man expresses himself in various ways: words are the means of literary language; numbers, of mathematical language; sounds, of musical language; and so on. Each one is specific and corresponds to equally specific needs.

The fact that we need varied means of expression is a clear indication that they are not equivalent to one another.

Each one appeals to different sensory, intellectual, and emotional receptors, from which it follows that there exists a real impossibility of translating one of these languages into another. Furthermore, what would be the use of translating music into logical thoughts? In music, says Combarieu, the expression is obtained by means of sound-feelings (*sensations musicales*) and not by means of concepts.[1]

Music is a language that speaks, in musical terms, of a specific musical thought, to the specifically musical sensitivity of man.

This does not mean that music has no meaning whatsoever, as has been said by some: it only means that music has a musical meaning, and not a literary meaning. Music finds a response only in those persons possessing a musical sense in a greater or lesser degree. It is just as impossible to translate music into words as to translate Cervantes into mathematical equations.

On the other hand, it is notorious that certain emotions or states of mind evoke in the composer himself, or in the audience, musical as well as plastic or literary images in many ways equivalent. We may say the Beethoven Pastoral Symphony does not pretend to be a description as in a series of tableaux. It simply means that the composer could have said: "When I wrote this music I was under the influence of the emotions of the countryside." That is the case, indeed, with all the titled music of Claude Debussy.

It would be good to note, also, that we cannot discard program music just because it is that. If we often do, it is rather because it is not very good music in itself. On the other hand, if the music contains solid musical values, what do we care whether it tries to be programmatic?

Generally speaking, movie music is not the best in history; but if written by a great composer, we would probably not despise it for being movie music. After all, Stravinsky's ballets—to mention a specific instance—are program music, whether they are the various rites of spring, the desperation of Petrouchka, or Orpheus looking for Eurydice; and what wonderful music! Someone may dismiss Debussy as "programmatic"; programmatic or not, what marvellous music —with or without the moon, the terraces, the night's perfumes, or the golden fish!

The creative artist is a transformer, transforming everything into an artistic language, translating it into his particular artistic language. A composer transforms, in terms of music, whatever he absorbs from the outside and whatever he is congenitally; he depicts his present moment in his music, so that, in reality, all music is autobiographical.

Whatever a human being does (thought, feeling, or action), whether it is art or the simple acts of everyday life, is a reflection of his personal tastes and needs, and a direct result of the circumstances of his surroundings. Everything we do is an outcome of our being, whether it is recorded in words, in music, in pictures, or not recorded at all.

At this very point we have to consider the question of dehumanized art, which furthermore should offer a good basis for future discussions about new trends in music.

It is generally accepted that art began by being mimetic, imitating human sentiments and emotions, and we have statements to the effect that in the Middle Ages (though scholastic counterpoint was the exception) the norm had not changed: "Melody ought to imitate the ideas and sentiments that are the object of song; to be, at the time, tranquil, to imitate calmness; joyful, to imitate joy; sad, to imitate mourning." [2] The principle is still valid for Mozart and eighteenth-century music in general. The nineteenth century professed the art-confession at its highest level, art as "extract of life"; the work of art was "a fiction of human realities." The twentieth century, in its turn, brought new and varied viewpoints that Mallarmé, Satie, and Debussy foresaw from their peculiar positions in the nineteenth century. They threw the first stones against heavily autobiographical art: "Life is one thing; Poetry or Music another." Art-purists *à outrance* would like to convince the world that art and life are completely detached entities. However, the clear position taken by Ortega y Gasset[3] in 1925 is still valid. The twentieth century, he says, has developed a "predominant propensity to dehumanize art; to avoid live forms; to try to manage so that a work of art would be solely a work of art; to consider art as a play; to tend to light, ironic positions; to elude falseness and to achieve perfect finish; and, lastly, not to take things too seriously, and avoid transcendental postures."

From these propensities we have seen the emergence of innumerable labels of formalistic art, and various *rétours* to the past in a modern light.

It would be impossible for even recalcitrant art-purists to give solidly grounded support to a thesis of thorough dehumanization. But we are bound to conclude that the essential springs of art have moved from the deep bottoms of human, thick emotion, to the higher levels of intellect and finer sentiments. In short, where we wanted before to be "human, all too human," now we are human in spite of ourselves.

However, perhaps we have a better approach to the matter, and here we come back to the beginning, and close our circuit. It is not precisely that we want art to be dehumanized; it is, rather, that we have come up to a higher state in the development of our specific musical sense, and we are, more and more, capable of a specific musical enjoyment. (I speak of music. The same would apply to the other arts.) Sounds, and their particular relationships, stimulate a specific sense in us, the musical sense, having nothing to do with ideas as such, with logical thoughts, with literary images, with plastic or colored sensations, with poetic metaphors, with sadness or joy, with everyday contingencies, or anything else.

The esthetic sense (being specifically musical, plastic, or literary) is just another sense like the five we already recognize. It must have an organ, as sight has eyes and hearing ears, though we do not know yet where it is located. But the center of gravity of music is changing from the extramusical to the musical.

I would like to mention, in this respect, a very personal experience. In my early youth I had of course my period of "human, all too human," and I used to listen to Chopin and Beethoven with a high sentimental pressure within me. I listen to Beethoven and Chopin now, and nothing of the sort happens. While people still talk of Chopin's wailings and Beethoven's sublime passions, I now listen and hear only music; music that does not evoke, or provoke, any extramusical thoughts or emotions. So, undoubtedly, the new approach not only proves to be a fact from the standpoint of the composer, but also from the standpoint of the listener. We are being educated to listen to music with a purely musical intention, and the growth of this capacity parallels the extent to which we develop our musical sense.

On first acquaintance—as I said—I thought I should, somehow, have to introduce myself, and I have first made some comments about the composer in general, the better to consider later the cultural position of our Latin American countries vis-à-vis the Occident.

To facilitate matters, I will speak of Latin America as one single, vast country, because of the common background of all the states concerned.

The evaluation of America and of the American man by the Europeans, biologically, sociologically, and culturally, has been, as you all know, matter for long discussions. Ever since the first appraisals made by the Spanish conquerors and by the discoverer himself, which, on the whole, were understanding of the situation, the discussions about America have been endless and, mostly, hostile.

From the basic standpoint of a naturalist, Buffon said in the eighteenth century: "There is, then, in the combination of elements and other physical causes, something contrary to the aggrandizement of living nature in this new world: there are obstacles to the development and perhaps to the formation of the great life-germs; even those which, subject to kind influences in a different climate, have achieved their full form and their complete extension, shrink and dwindle under this avaricious sky, and in this empty land." So, according to Buffon's genetics, all "living nature" was thus thwarted in America, including man who in this desolate world was only a "powerless automaton." [4]

Latin America was for Europe the source of an incredible wealth; and when the numerous Iberian colonies began to have a certain personality of their own, in the eighteenth century, America began to be a cause of some jealousy and concern. It did not make much sense to compare Europe with America, two different things in themselves, and furthermore there were very likely deficiencies in actual data about this continent.

After Buffon, hundreds of commentators followed in all fields: statesmen and scientists, philosophers and journalists. The theoretical dispute paralleled the grave politico-sociological dissensions that ended in the independence of the Iberian colonies and the isolationist declaration of President Monroe.

At the beginning of the nineteenth century America was free, its major problem being ethnico-cultural integration. Three hundred years of cruel and merciless colonialism had not exterminated the Indians. Not only were they still there physically, but they were, to a large degree, faithful to their noble past. Accused of "frigidity and lack of sensitiveness" —in the words of Kant—they possessed, however, an old

Indian tradition, a tradition of beauty and magnificence, of refinement and sensitivity. It is no wonder that this world was not understood. The superb, abstract, formalistic creations of Olmec, Toltec, Mayan, and Aztec art could not possibly go along with Hellenic beauty, the classicism and naturalism of the Renaissance, the baroque of the eighteenth century, or the romanticism of the nineteenth. The European man could not possibly see anything but monstrousness in ancient Mexican sculpture and painting. It was not until the swift, multiple evolution of European art during the first twenty-five years of this century, which assimilated all possible past and present idioms and styles, that the Western world arrived at a position where understanding was possible. It is therefore quite understandable that the Indians were accused of savagery and lack of sensitivity.

It is to be noted that while Indian science and technology, and the general development of knowledge, lagged hundreds of years behind Europe, the plastic arts had attained a high degree of advancement. If we call Mexican and Peruvian art "primitive" we should first agree on what we mean by this term. If we mean incipient, primeval, undeveloped, the word is inappropriate to designate precolonial art. Probably developing in a direct line from the stone ages, Indian artists followed for several centuries a long course of slow and steady evolution, until they reached, by themselves, the highest stages of formalistic art: symbolic, decorative, constructivist, which sometimes makes one think of cubism.

One is amazed at the terrific amount of thought and concentration given for centuries by these peoples to the creation of works of art, and the inquisitive spirit with which it was done. There were no stereotyped forms or patterns of any kind; among thousands of pieces that time and destruction have been good enough to let us have and see, there are no two alike.

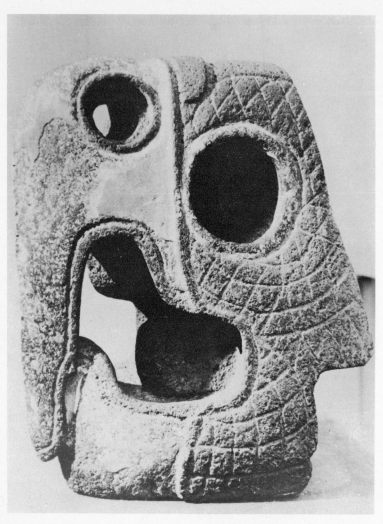

HEAD OF A MACAW. Toltec civilization, A.D. 800–1200,
Xochicalco, State of Morelos, Mexico

The sculptors of those masterpieces were true, great masters; if their names did not survive, as did those of Phidias and Michelangelo, they must nevertheless have had names, individual names.

The Indian made his way through a land of insane geography: the interminable desert of the plateaus and the devouring jungle of the tropics. Yes, on one hand the inclement, dry, "avaricious skies" in the desolate landscape of the *mesetas,* and on the other the lush, monstrous tropic, where man must compete with ferocious rivals of all sizes. How many scientists, statesmen, and travelers of present and past have warned the world against the tropics—perhaps with reason. I think differently: having lived a long while in the tropics, I find them enormously healthy and encouraging. They are so much so that all sorts of creatures of the animal and vegetable kingdoms hurry down there to enjoy their revitalizing strength. Then the matter resolves itself to a sheer question of outright competition with mosquitoes, scorpions, tigers, and lions, who also wish to enjoy the endless advantages of the tropics. I myself have found nothing more stimulating than the shadows in the forest, the soothing breeze of the twilight, and the calm of the tropical nights.

In their millenarian fight against nature, the American Indians developed a very elaborate religion. An infinite number of rites and ceremonies were the reason for the sculpture, architecture, and painting which nowadays we call art. This situation, of course, is no different from that of the Chinese, Hindus, Assyrians, Babylonians, Chaldeans, or Egyptians, who never intended to create art; the Aztecs never even had the word *beauty* in their vocabulary. However, it matters little; they all created immeasurable beauty, which means, at the very least, that you do not have to know anything about beauty in order to create it. It is very healthy to arrive at this realization, particularly in these days of such elaborate techniques and super-techniques, meant expressly to create beauty. Art is made by the esthetic sense. Small children do not know that they have five senses, but they see, and hear, and smell, and taste, and feel just as well.

For us in Latin America, who have lived the life of our countries, a study of the past is not necessary. The past is present. We, for instance, knew of abstractionism and so-called "primitivism" long before such trends were the fashion in Europe. They are in our eyes and ears, and the legacy came directly to our hearts. Indeed, a country like Mexico, especially the Mexico of my youth, forty-five years ago, creates in one the feeling of man's association with the earth for thousands of years. This link with the remote past is deep and subconscious. At this point certain recollections of my childhood occur to me. I was a small child and heard the grown-ups speak of Christopher Columbus and the discovery of America. I was confused; I could not quite understand. And I remember once telling them: "All right, but what do you mean by that? What is it that he discovered? Is America anything to be discovered? Weren't we already here?"

There were, then, the first discoverers, Indians entering America some ten thousand years ago, and the second discoverers, Spaniards, commanded by Christopher Columbus, some five hundred years ago. The former made their own closed, continental world, and certainly would have taken a lot of time to discover Europe by themselves. The latter wanted a world wide and open, and there lies their incontestable superiority. The former were content with a closed world, and the latter were not so content.

In those parts of the American continent where no important previous culture was in force, there was a transplantation of the European, under varied circumstances of great interest, not to be discussed here. In places where the original American culture had attained a considerable development, where there was a state, a social life, a well-structured concept of family relations, an organized religion, an incipient science and technology, and superb manifestations of fine arts—though not conceived or created as such—the meeting of the second discoverers with the previous ones determined a transculturation, a difficult one, through a somewhat painful and slow process. There was a great deal to regret about the conquerors, but there was indeed a positive side also. The Spaniards have been a heroic race —enterprising, noble, imaginative. And our peoples, nowadays, are something more than the summing up of the two ingredients. Alfonso Reyes has said:

"From that moment [of their independence] the former colonies were left in the category of societies that had not created a culture, but had received it ready-made from all the cultural centers of the world. By an understandable process, the entire cultural heritage of the world became their patrimony on terms of equality. Their culture, however, as far as our peoples are concerned, always stemming from the Hispanic source, broadened with the absorption of all foreign contributions, at times as an act of deliberate hostility and reaction against the former mother country, but more often out of conviction, and as the result of an attitude of universalism." [5]

This direction toward the universal can be the best answer to the extremism of *Indigenistas* and *Hispanistas*. The former claim that everything ought to be gotten from old native sources, and the latter, seeing no values in the native, prefer to stick exclusively to the Spanish. Both positions are vulnerable because they postulate a limitation. Why limit ourselves in one way or the other? Besides, it is not altogether a matter of choice; it goes as it goes.

In the field of music our Latin American countries have often made an effort toward a national style. Nationalist composers have used folk material as a basis for their compositions. To try to be "national" seemed a good way to try to be personal. This has been very much in favor in Mexico and many other Latin American countries ever since the days of independence. It would be all right, but there are two or three disadvantages. To use folk material as a permanent expedient would be indeed limiting. Second, if the composer uses folk themes to the exclusion of his own, he will be giving up a very important part of his creative function. Third, the fact that a Mexican or Brazilian composer uses national folk themes does not guarantee his acquiring a style of his own, or even a "national" style.

Now, it is true that our colonial life was somewhat passive; that our life did not begin to be really active until our independence. It is true, also, that if things are handed down to us ready-made instead of being developed independently, we do not fully integrate our tradition.

However, in the integration of our musical tradition there are some interesting situations. True enough, Latin American musical culture does not have in its past any Bachs or Beethovens; Latin American countries so far have given to the world—in music or art in general—neither more nor less than what they could possibly have given. There may be impatient or pessimistic critics; but our countries have had a very peculiar historic development within which, with all its handicaps and contradictions, there seems to be a very consistent line of progressive development. We can trace back a very well-articulated past of our own. The Indian music, before the Conquest, at least in Mexico and Peru, had passed from the pentatonic to the diatonic and was definitely modal, in its own way, though without any established system. I myself have very often heard Indian chants or dances, or both, in the Dorian and Phrygian modes that, due to the special places and circumstances, seemed to be of purely Indian origin. Furthermore, Gregorian chant was spread all over the country by the Catholic Church; and it would be well to remember that religion and religious rites permeated the whole of life. Through the Church, again, we got a large dose of polyphony, so that Indian modal monody, Gregorian chant, and polyphony, united, provided all kinds of music: sacred, profane, and pagan. Somehow the Indians have a talent for polyphony, as well as for polyrhythm, or for both, manifested in much of the music of the country. Then, for long stretches of time, during the seventeenth and eighteenth centuries, there were church composers of minor rank, but thoroughly learned, who composed masses for the regular services after the style of the music of Handel and Mozart. This had a tremendous impact, and, again, the immense popularity of religious ceremonies brought this music within the reach of every living creature. Together with this, the Spanish songs and dances, implanted by the missionaries ever since the beginning of the sixteenth century, created a musical atmosphere of amazing scope; it may be said that the missionaries constantly preached and taught by musical means to cope with previous Indian uses. Now to complete the picture.

Learned musical institutions existed before the Conquest in Mexico and Peru, regular schools of music and dance for the religious cults and the army; and it goes without saying that the newcomers had also to cope with this. We have reports of Spanish music teachers as far back as Bernal Díaz del Castillo (a Conquistador himself), and the Catholic Church saw to it that music was taught formally everywhere, so that when the first conservatories were established in the nineteenth century, there was sufficient background for them.

It follows from the foregoing that ever since the beginning composers have been much in demand in Latin America, the best customer having been the Church. Many of them came from Spain, and some from Italy; but notices from early chroniclers give accounts of remarkable composers of pure Indian blood.

At the outset of the nineteenth century the first signs of musical nationalism appeared, and efforts in this direction have never ceased. Conservatories took on, more and more, the shape of their European models, and opera and public concerts began to be common.

Toward the middle of the century the whole Latin American continent was overwhelmed with Italian opera. All the capital and many provincial cities built opera houses; Italian opera companies triumphed everywhere. Characteristic of the composers of the time was the *musique de salon* so much in favor, and the brilliant fantasies for piano, *alla* Liszt or Gottschalk,[6] using Italian opera themes or national folk tunes.

Toward the end of the second third of the century Beethoven began to be known and played. It was not so easy to imitate Beethoven as it had been to follow closely the style of Italian opera and showy piano fantasies, so that while admiration was great, the actual effect was not very noticeable in the music of Latin American composers, who were not yet ready to attack the large musical forms: sonata, symphony, and the like. The last third of the century saw a profusion of small pieces, still *musique de salon:* gavottes, mazurkas, *feuilles d'album,* and, indeed, waltzes and marches, all coming out of diverse models such as Mozart or Chopin. The impact of Chopin, it goes without saying, was devastating; but his superior, highly developed harmony could not possibly be imitated.

From this world of beginnings, however, something was taking shape: the habanera, originating in the contredanse, is a good instance at hand;[7] and so is the tango, both—habanera and tango—having become universal. In Mexico, Cuba, Colombia, Venezuela, Brazil, Argentina, Chile, and Peru, very remarkable waltzes and marches, and innumerable dances of triple blood—Spanish, Indian, and Negro—were already pieces of intrinsic musical value, with a character all their own. In all this development, the semiclassical and the semipopular still borrowed from one another. The serious composer, on the other hand, gave signs, at the dawn of the twentieth century, of a more mature personality. Attempts were made in the larger forms: sonata, concerto, quartet. Though definitely of local importance only, there were already some pieces that stood on their own feet.

At this point, an impending local socio-political crisis gave a strong impetus to the already advanced process of cultural integration in Mexico: it was the Revolution. It shook Mexico to her foundations; but other world-wide factors—World War I and the phenomenal widening of world communication—were of quick, far-reaching effect in all Latin America.

It is quite obvious that no art work of truly superior rank can be expected from a country that has not reached a minimum level of cultural integration, though the level, of course, is flexible. It is all right to speak of epochs, and periods and historic currents, and nations, and transculturation. It is all right to get very sociological. But what makes up society, after all? Individuals.

In this matter of individuality our Lord has been very whimsical. Nicaragua is one of the smaller and more hard-up of our "underdeveloped" Latin American countries; and Nicaragua has given the highest, greatest creative genius yet born below the Río Grande: the poet Rubén Darío.

Art is, essentially, an individual expression. The individual is molded in some way by the sociological group or nation he comes from. Every individual is so molded, and in that way he expresses his tradition and collective characteristics; but the tradition and the collective characteristics express themselves through an individual, not through collectivity itself. This is always true, not only in the case of art music, but also in so-called ethnological expressions, folk art and the like. An anonymous song is collectively inherited for generations and generations, but originally it was composed by one single man, even though with the rolling of time it has suffered deformations—deformations which, in their turn, have been the contributions of an infinite number of single individuals. Also, we speak, for instance, of German Music, or German Art Music, as of a national, collective thing. Well, the seventeenth, eighteenth, and nineteenth centuries— three hundred years of German music—can be reduced to a few individual names: Bach and Handel, Haydn and Mozart, Beethoven, Wagner and Brahms, and a couple more, if you like.

So we come to an obvious conclusion: the great art, the great music of, let us say, Brazil or Mexico—just as that of Germany or France—will not be achieved merely by reaching a certain historical, sociological status, or by means of nationalistic techniques, or by any techniques whatever, but by the talent or genius of individual composers, born in such lands.

We are, in fact, confronted with a problem of individuals: the selection and intensive education of individuals of rare and unusual gifts, whose talent ought to be highly trained and specialized. (By highly specialized training I do not mean highly isolated laboratories.)

Coming to the end of these comments we arrive at the realization that the case of a Latin American composer is, basically, no different from the case of one from any other land. But let us have no doubt: every land exerts on its men, whether they sense it or not, its own telluric influence.

It is good to let our minds ascend to higher and higher levels, to geometric planes and abstractions; but we must not altogether renounce our part as live actors, or at least curious spectators, in the concrete play of reality.

II

Art as Communication

We, as social beings, are always facing a problem of understanding, and always looking for means of achieving it. We want others to make themselves accessible to us just as much as we want to make ourselves accessible to them. This is a mutual commerce in which we want to give just as much as to receive; in which egoism and altruism shift in contradictory interplay as we instinctively try to keep the proper balance. For we want to be alone just as much as we want to be with others.

Alone we are, anyway, in many areas: helplessly alone in many innermost circumstances. Yet how frightened we are at the very idea of being locked out from the rest of the world, our eyes blind, our ears deaf, our mouth shut. It is disquieting to watch the semimute world of animal nature: the admirable bearing of a horse, sparkling eyes, nervous ears and skin; agile, firm movements; an air of alertness and intelligence; and yet, silent, alone, isolated.

They must have been infelicitous, those dark, remote days when men wanted to express more than they were able to; and yet the anguish of isolation brought about the urge for communication. Language comes from anguish, strife, urge.

Far be it from me to attempt a survey of current ideas on the subject of the origin of language. But I would like to recall certain fundamental traits of the problem of communication. Art is as much a means of communication as language; they have a common origin and have served identical purposes. Anthropologists agree on the basic fact that human speech was evolved from animal cries and that emotional, volitional, and sensory experiences were conveyed just as much by language proper as by early art expressions. "The sounds uttered by birds offer in several respects the earliest analogy to language. The first attempts to sing may be compared to the imperfect endeavor of a child to babble . . . language owes its origin . . . to man's own instinctive cries, aided by signs and gestures . . . language has been unconsciously developed in many steps." [1]

At this moment we can see the intermediate steps by looking at some species in lower stages of evolution. "The wild parent-species of the dog expressed their feelings by cries of various kinds. With the domesticated dog we have the bark of eagerness, as in the chase; that of anger, as when growling; the yelp or howl of despair, as when shut up; the baying at night; the bark of joy, as when starting on a walk with his master; and the very distinct one of demand or supplication, as when wishing for a door or window to be opened." [2]

So we, in domestication, have learned to speak and to sing, to dance and to act, to paint and to carve. For what else has the long, painful run of civilization been if not a

long, painful process of domestication, which we still undergo as long as we live?

– Domestication has been the process of advancing in the
drive to understand others (communication) and project
ourselves in the form of speech and art (self-expression).
⌐ Thus communication and self-expression stand respectively for the social and the individual, the altruistic and
the egoistic, in a well-amalgamated mixture.

It is quite understandable that at first all forms of communication had a utilitarian purpose. Language, of course;
but music and painting and dance—in their incipient phases
—were also utilitarian, as in these early stages art was an
agent of magic, and magic is nothing but a utilitarian
expedient.

Nevertheless, however utilitarian, these forms of expression had in themselves all the characteristics of art, since
they came from, and appealed to, the esthetic sense of the
individual. The sensitivity to esthetic values was not a
phenomenon of which early man was aware, but the beauty
of the earliest paintings, chants, dances, and sculptures
prove that, consciously or not, an esthetic sense was there.

Now, philology and semantics explain to us how language
developed thought at the same rate and, *au fur et à mesure,*
that thought developed language. So we may say that art
developed our esthetic sense in the same parallel fashion
that our esthetic sense developed art. This, of course, is an
eternal flux and reflux that unquestionably constitutes an
evolution. Does this evolution constitute progress? How
can we doubt that in the equation speech-thought there
has been progress? Has it been so, however, in the equation
art-esthetic sense?

When things are of an objective order we can speak with
some certainty of progress. There has been progress in the
fact that we now go from New York to California in a
Diesel train, not in a stagecoach; in the fact that we have

concrete instead of mud roads. But when things are of a subjective nature, it is quite another matter. Can we speak of progress in art?

Stravinsky's warning on the subject is quite to the point: "A much abused word," he says, ". . . evolution which has been revered as a goddess—a goddess who turned out to be somewhat of a tramp, let it be said in passing, even to having given birth to a little bastard myth that looks very much like her and that has been named Progress, with a capital P. . . ." [3]

Victor Hugo, too, made the point very clearly and expressed it beautifully. "L'Art suprême est la région des égaux. Le chef-d'œuvre est adéquat au chef-d'œuvre." ("Supreme art is the region of equals. One masterpiece is equivalent to the other.") And he goes on:

> Like water which, heated to one hundred degrees, cannot increase in heat or rise further, human thought reaches in certain men its fullest intensity. Aeschylus, Job, Phidias, Isaiah, St. Paul, Juvenal, Dante, Michelangelo, Rabelais, Cervantes, Shakespeare, Rembrandt, Beethoven, and still others, mark the hundred degrees of genius.
> The human spirit has a summit.
> This summit is the ideal.

He continues:

> Among human things, and as a human thing, art is a singular exception.
> The beauty of all things here on earth lies in their capacity to improve themselves; everything is endowed with this property: to grow, increase, strengthen, spread, advance, to be worth more today than yesterday. . . . The beauty of art consists in not being susceptible of improvement. . . .
> A masterpiece exists once and for all. The first poet to arrive, arrives at the summit. You will climb after him, just as high, no higher. Ah! your name is Dante, be it so: but this one is called Homer.
> Progress—the goal constantly removed, the stage always renewed —has changes of horizon. The ideal, none.
> Now, progress is the motor of science; the ideal is the generator of art.

This explains why improvement is proper to science, but not at all proper to art.

One scholar causes another to be forgotten; a poet does not make another fall into oblivion.

. . . They succeed, they do not replace, one another. The beautiful does not hunt the beautiful. Neither wolves nor masterworks devour each other.

. . . Art is not susceptible of intrinsic progress. From Phidias to Rembrandt there is motion, not progress. The frescoes of the Sistine Chapel do absolutely nothing to the metopes of the Parthenon. Go back as far as you wish, from the Palace of Versailles to the Schloss of Heidelberg, from the Schloss of Heidelberg to Notre-Dame of Paris, from Notre-Dame of Paris to the Alhambra, from the Alhambra to Santa Sophia, from Santa Sophia to the Coliseum, from the Coliseum to the Propylaea, from the Propylaea to the Pyramids; you can retreat through the centuries, but you do not retreat in art. The Pyramids and the Iliad remain in the foreground.

Masterpieces have a level, the same for all, the Absolute.[4]

It is to be noted that, whereas Hugo insistently mentions painters, poets, sculptors, and architects, he hardly refers to musicians. This may very well be of no special significance, but, in any event, we can approach the subject and put to ourselves the following question: does Mozart constitute progress over Bach; Beethoven over Mozart; Brahms over Beethoven; Debussy over Brahms; and so forth?

Indeed the answer is no; there is no progress from one to the other; they are all equally great and immortal. For there is no doubt that this question of progress is somehow linked with that of immortality: if the chain is one of immortals, there is no progress.

Is there, then, any probability that the chain of immortality will be broken one day?

Predictions are always hypothetical, and on such shifting ground as this any hypothesis would be senseless. All we can do here is try to work out certain general considerations.

Why did we start the supposed chain with Bach? This ought to have some meaning. Is it arbitrary, or a matter of personal choice? The Renaissance was a very remarkable era, abounding in notable musical achievements, in which flourished men of great genius—Monteverdi, Victoria, Palestrina—whom, however, we are not accustomed to calling immortal. Can we call immortals those musicians preceding Palestrina, Victoria, Monteverdi? I have never heard anyone call them by that name.

It is quite clear that we give the name immortal to those men of outstanding genius whom we most admire. Does this mean, then, that before Bach there were no men of outstanding genius? That I will answer categorically: it is impossible to state with authority that Bach was the first man of genius in the history of occidental music.

The fact remains that, while there undoubtedly were geniuses before Bach, we start our chain of immortals with him, and call no composers immortals before him. This plainly indicates that with Bach a new era of music begins, which we put on a higher level than those that preceded it.

We can be certain that from Bach to our day—two hundred and fifty years, roughly—all the great masters are immortals: this means, definitely, that we do not admit any progress within this period of time. But does it not imply that we see progress from the mortal composers to the immortal ones?

If, supposing the impossible, we were able to listen to the music of lyres and aulos as played in an Athenian Olympiad, we would be absolutely fascinated. But second and third acquaintance with it would completely change this attitude; and very likely our interest in it would become purely historical.

I do not know whether we could reasonably say that if so deep a gap exists between yesterday and today, the gap might become equally great or greater between today and tomorrow. If we do not call the masters of more than three hundred years ago immortal, are our present immortals

going to be so named in the three hundred years to come?
We noted before that Hugo confined his statements to poetry, literature, and the plastic arts. This might have been so simply because he was not thinking of music. It is, however, quite obvious that there are not, in music, ranking contemporaries of Homer or Dante. It has been said that music is slow and moves behind the other arts, but looking objectively at the matter we may say either that music is slower or music is faster. The other arts are still within the cycle of Aeschylus and Phidias; they have not moved much in twenty-five hundred years. Music long ago surpassed the cycle of Pindarus and Pythagoras, having moved along incessantly. In twenty-five hundred years music has undergone innumerable and often violent changes, the result being that painters, sculptors, and poets have lasted longer than musicians. Whereas great master poets, painters, sculptors, architects have lasted thousands of years, great master musicians have only lasted hundreds of years. Great master musicians burn quickly. Is this going to change in the future? The course of history is pretty consistent: we cannot be entirely sure that our great names of today, our Bachs and Debussys, will not be just historical names in the three hundred (or three thousand) years to come.

I mentioned that, in developing art through the generations, men had developed in parallel fashion their esthetic sense. If Beethoven's Ninth Symphony is a far more complex organism than any musical piece of twenty-five hundred years ago, it is because modern man is more complex also. We move toward more intricate and highly organized forms and expressions in the same measure that we become so. Whether this course toward the more complex may or may not be called progress does not alter the fact in itself; I myself, for the sake of clarity, would not be afraid to call it that. Furthermore, there exist palpable indications of the development (or progress) of man's esthetic sense in that the earliest artistic expressions in the course of time finally became works of art proper.

Early art was utilitarian. The earliest known documents, the marvelous paleolithic paintings and drawings in the caves of southern France and northern Spain, were the "instrument of a magical technique and as such had a thoroughly pragmatic function aimed entirely at direct economic objectives." [5]

Or, as a more cautious authority puts it: ". . . since the subjects represented are, with few exceptions, the food animals of these Ice-age peoples, it would seem that they were depicted to insure a plentitude of the animal or the actual securing of it in the hunt. Both motivations may very well have been behind the art." [6]

Nothing different can be said of the stone, bone, or ivory amulets, and sculpture as such, that have come to us from those remotest times; or of the magic chants and songs, as we know them among primitive peoples of our day, designed to appease the bad spirits and propitiate the good ones. The principles of magic—imitation and repetition—were the basis for the technique of this early art, although such marvelous paintings as those in the Altamira caves are eloquent proof of early man's esthetic sense.

Sensitive, then, to esthetic values, early man felt the exceptionally expressive power of such artistic media, and it was due to that very realization that he conceded a supernatural power to painting, music, and sculpture.

Speech, of more clearly utilitarian purpose, is said to have been, however, of a very definite poetic origin. Gianbattista Vico speaks of the "first men," "children of nascent mankind," whose senses are "their sole way of knowing things." And he goes on: ". . . poetic wisdom; the first of the gentile world, must have begun with a metaphysic not rational and not abstract like that of learned men now, but felt and imagined as that of these first men must have been, who without power of ratiocination, were all robust in sense, and vigorous in imagination."

Poetic wisdom comes from the senses and the imagination of nascent mankind. According to him, figures of speech, tropes, as we now understand them, preceded speech proper.

He proceeds to explain in detail how metaphors were the natural expression for the primitive, unintelligent man of simple, egocentric nature:

"*Homo non Intelligendo Fit Omnia.* Man becomes all things by not understanding them; when he does not understand he makes the things out of himself, and becomes them, by transforming himself into them. And so, he called mouth any opening, lip for the rim of a vase, foot for end, heart for center. And synecdoches such as head for man or person was due to the fact that in the forests only the head of a man could be seen from a distance; and *tectum,* roof, came to mean a whole house because in the first times a covering sufficed for a house." [7]

Thus, tropes were "the necessary poetic modes of expression of "first men." "Speech in verse" came first, and "prose speech" came later, he says.

One way or the other, we may say that there was much of the utilitarian in art and much of art in the utilitarian—a single trunk of expression. However, in the course of time, things did develop toward specialization. Utilitarian means of communication became more utilitarian, and artistic means of communication became more and more properly called so. Starting from the very same trunk, two branches were little by little strengthening their own peculiar characteristics.

But when and how is it that utilitarian communication and art communication finally separated?

It is one thing to play and sing beautiful music—no matter how beautiful—for hours and hours, as in magic chants; and it is quite another matter to create a form using musical materials.

⌐ Creation of form results from another urge, a different type of psychological need. It is not so much the need for communication as it is the impulse to project our ego. It is also a manner of giving way to our natural mimetic condition: we live in a universe of creation, and we ourselves want to be able to create in our turn, too; we ourselves have a given form, and we want to give birth to creatures of a given shape, also.

The difference between singing or playing endlessly and creating a form is simply a matter of establishing physical limits: as soon as there are given frontiers, the work of art appears. The first condition of a work of art is that it be limited in space or time. We can call "art" the endless playing of a Balinese gamelan, but we cannot properly call it a work of art. So, as soon as music is limited in time there is form, and we have the basic element of a work of art. Then form has to correspond to our tastes and feelings, and we endow it with a given morphology of its own. We want to make a creature with certain parts of its own that would make a coherent whole, because we ourselves rejoice in the contemplation of a unity. Man loves unities. That is how form has become the *sine qua non* of art as we conceive it nowadays.

Indeed, the Homeric poems are not a beginning, but the culminating point of ages of disorderly epics. And Homer was the first to introduce some order, having in view the need for unity and form: an organized anatomy.

The advent of form brought with it the consciousness of the artistic creation and, in the course of time, the necessity of developing and perfecting techniques. For a long while, techniques—as such—prevailed, and art forms became more and more stereotyped. Techniques were the means and rules for creating art and art-forms, and this was the apogee of the artisan. Thus, the individual was truly in a second plane. There he remained for some time, but he could not forever. The nineteenth century (in music, with Beethoven) saw the individual coming definitely to the foreground; the era of the great individual creation began. Here was no longer the artisan—here was the inspired artist. From now on it was not only technique but individual inspiration that would make the work of art possible.

And here begins a more or less latent or open controversy about the actual meaning—or should we say place?—of technique and inspiration in the creative process.

Nowadays there seems to be a certain tendency to oppose craftsmanship to inspiration, and to look down at so-called inspiration with a certain disdain. It would seem as if inspiration were unelegant and something to be a bit ashamed of. On the other hand, a more common idea seems to be that inspiration is provided by God as a special grace at a given moment, a sort of miracle that comes in the form of a divine spark. To others, "inspired" music would necessarily be the equivalent of some sort of "sentimental" music.

Very likely, however, inspiration has nothing to do with sentimentality or esoterics. When a man sets himself to creative work, he will certainly have to put into it the best of whatever faculties he has. This is true of inventors or research scientists as well as creative artists.

The creating man has to concentrate, concentrate thoroughly, so that in this light inspiration is sheer concentration. Concentration is the most propitious state for creation. How can one create, invent, originate, when one's mind is busy with other thoughts or worries? One often hears stories of Chopin's sufferings and love worries being the basic inspiration for his music. It may very well be so, but at the time the man was actually composing there is no question that his mind could not possibly be occupied with anything else but music.

Inspiration is a state of spirit, a state of mind, and—why not?—a state of trance, of ecstasy (in its rigorous sense of being carried away), in which all the mental, psychic, and spiritual forces of the individual concur intensely for a single purpose, that of creating, composing, or investigating: a total concentration of human faculties in a given direction. We do not call all cases of concentration inspiration, but all cases of inspiration involve concentration.

Indeed, inspiration cannot be a chronic state; it is, rather, an acute state. It can be of shorter or longer duration, but would be impossible to maintain for long stretches of time. Like any other acute state, it is rare, and implies a total mobilization of man's faculties which tires and wears him out. (In the same way, a weight lifter, mobilizing all the strength of the muscles in his body, cannot be lifting weights all the time without interruption.) For this reason, perhaps, it has been conceded a divine or esoteric nature.

However, inspiration is not fortuitous. The capacity to concentrate all mental and emotional faculties at a given moment is one that develops and improves through function. We invoke inspiration or, rather, we provoke it when we set ourselves to work. In order to concentrate one has to forget. As soon as complete forgetfulness of everything else is achieved, the muse, docile and unpretentious, comes and stays.

More confusion has been derived from the fact that we are accustomed to hearing of "inspired composers," such as Verdi, as opposed to "intellectual composers," such as Stravinsky. If it is true that Igor Stravinsky manipulates his given materials far more than Giuseppe Verdi, that does not imply that the latter is more inspired than the former. Everybody knows that in the creative process there are two states: the unconscious and the conscious. There has been a good deal of speculation about this, but nobody can establish with certitude where or when the unconscious ends and the conscious begins. Somehow, what has been called "inspirational" corresponds to the unconscious, and what has been called "intellectual" refers to the conscious. But, seemingly, that which has been called "conscious" or "intellectual" requires just as much invention as the other part; and to what extent is invention a conscious process? That would be, certainly, difficult to determine with any degree of precision. I am inclined to think that the successful manipulation of given musical materials requires the same kind of inventional aptitudes as the invention of the materials themselves. It is all a matter of inclination: Verdi was not inclined to manipulate his materials; rather, he used fresh materials all the time, and they flowed and flowed miraculously as from an inexhaustible fountain; Stravinsky is inclined to manipulate his materials, and his manipulations flow and flow miraculously as from an inexhaustible source. And who would dare to say that Stravinsky is right and Verdi wrong, or vice versa?

Many people are inclined to think that technique is everything: it is a general belief that in order to become a composer you learn a technique and you learn to compose. In a sense, of course, that is true. But the technique that one gets from books is another man's technique; it is Palestrina's technique or a "serial" technique. That is all right as a way to start; at the beginning of his career Beethoven used Haydn techniques, but from that point on he developed his own. A composer wants to make his own music, and that can only be achieved by developing his own technique. We have to know the particular techniques of all the great masters well; first, to learn from them and, second, to avoid them consistently.

I am not at this point trying to write an essay on the way a composer should be taught. What I am trying to say is

that a technique should be something personal. Every great
composer has his own technique, and in many cases each
and every work of the same composer has followed a particular technique. If we understand technique as the sum
of technical means to express oneself, it will be clear that
everyone has to master such means by himself. This is a
matter of time and quantity of work: and *quantity* is an
essential element. We are used to thinking of quantity in a
pejorative sense—quantity as opposed to quality—but this
notion needs clarification. A pilot's mastery is measured in
terms of the quantity of hours of flight: so too can Beethoven's mastery be measured. If he had written three symphonies instead of nine—a pure matter of quantity—he
would not have reached the ever-increasing mastery of the
other six symphonies. If he had not worked consistently, the
supreme mastery of the Ninth would have never been
achieved. As the flyer's mastery is measured in terms of
quantity of flying hours, so Beethoven's can be measured
in terms of composing hours.

Technique cannot be handed to us ready made. We make
it, we develop it through years and years of functioning: a
writer by writing, a composer by composing, a painter by
painting—or a flyer by flying.

But the question is not only one of inspiration and technique. There are other essentials: the good or bad taste of
the man, and, above all, talent.

If we understand talent as a quality element, and functioning as a quantity element, we shall have to conclude
that there is a direct ratio between quantity and quality.
A change in quantity brings about a change in quality, it
has been said with much reason. The greater the number
of symphonies, the greater the change in their quality:
quantity in composing hours brought about the incredible
change in quality between the first and the ninth of the
Beethoven symphonies.

In the last analysis, talent is everything, not technique. We come back to inspiration, a concentration of all positive faculties, its only reason for existence being the specific musical talent.

We know of the many efforts directed toward denying the individual and the individual essence of artistic creation. For instance, the dictates to conform artistic production to given political principles are nothing but technical dictates: use tonic and dominant, tonality of C major, no distant modulations, use elemental melodies and elemental rhythmic patterns, and so on. This is, in fact, a return to artisanship in its worst possible form. The individual is frozen and cannot move from the techniques imposed upon him. Of a very similar nature is the attitude adopted by some musicians of the present relying basically on pre-established techniques. If I may give a definition, an artisan is the man who always follows pre-established techniques, whereas an artist is the man who always invents new techniques. Pre-established techniques cannot be followed without fettering man's creative drive, in the sense that creation implies newness.

In the course of time musicians passed from established to constantly renewed techniques. Techniques have to be renewed from one work to the other because at this point in the evolution of musical art we do not want "mass production"—symphonies all alike as are refrigerators or kitchen ware. In man's urge for creation there is implicit an element of saying new things. I said before that man loves unities. Man loves unities because he loves to differentiate. Man loves to differentiate because he himself, in the course of ages, has undergone a steady process of differentiation and specialization. So that art, as we finally have come to understand it, manifests itself in a unit with a character and a form of its own, with individuality. A man is an individual and wants to create individuals. In this way we are happy to emulate God, inasmuch as we ourselves rejoice in the creation of a new, individual piece of art.

The past stages of artisanship have corresponded to epochs of limitation of individual freedoms, which effected a corresponding subdual of the inquisitive spirit. For the creative spirit is by nature inquisitive; the more inquisitive, the more creative. I think it is not only by chance that the era of great individual creations in music started with the nineteenth century, when individual liberties and rights began to assert themselves. In fact, before the nineteenth century the whole history of man is one of subjection—subjection to kings, princes, feudal lords, or tribal leaders.

Creation in itself implies the exaltation of the individual. Not only unintelligent man "becomes all things," as I quoted before from Vico. He also says: "*Homo Intelligendo Fit Omnia;* man becomes all things by understanding them; when man understands he extends his mind and takes in things." [8] When the artist understands, he extends himself to new and unexpected areas; he sees more; he concentrates in himself and beauty becomes a revelation.

Egoism brings about concentration, for concentration implies loneliness; but loneliness brings about the urge to communicate with others, and egoism then dissolves into altruism.

By himself becoming "all things," the artist synthesizes, gives shape to new art forms, and thus attains communication with his fellow men.

III

Form in Music

The notion of form implies that of an entity—a being—a unity limited in space or time.

In fact, any existing thing has form, and we speak of the form of the whole, as well as of the form of the parts that constitute it. But form can be more or less individualized, more or less isolated. There is the form of a tree and the form of a human being, and there are vast forms of inanimate objects, rocks and mountains.

✳ Man finds in the universe all sorts of previously created forms; and himself forming part of that creation, he in turn pursues creation. In this pursuit man has developed all sorts of things to satisfy his needs, and thus has created art. ✳

As we now see it, art is a satisfaction to our esthetic needs. For some time, not so long ago, it was considered a

35

superfluous luxury. Now it seems that even politicians have to accept the fact that esthetic needs are important: as important as, let us say, nutrition. Looking at it objectively, after all, art is nothing but nutrition for our most complicated psycho-intellectual needs. A short time ago the Board of Education of the City of New York was accused of "waste and extravagance" in the building of schools, and its immediate reply was that it had "been careful to be economical without diminishing the esthetic quality" of the city's new schools.[1] As a matter of fact, if we compare the average house and office building of today with those of only fifty years ago, the difference is amazing in that esthetic requirements are now a major consideration. The overwhelming success of "interior decorators" and the incredible demand for painting, sculpture, and *objets d'art* for home decoration is another instance at hand, not to mention that if fifty years ago all well-to-do ladies and young ladies dressed elegantly, it is now a general practice for women of all social classes and ages to dress beautifully. Music—music of an elevated order—was not long ago the exclusive privilege of a few persons, whereas now, being within the reach of everyone, all seem to care for it.

The hunger for beauty, coming from an increasing esthetic need, has led to the creation of art and art-forms. Art and art-forms, I said in a previous chapter, are not quite the same thing; they correspond to the general and the specific. To say *art* is to refer to a generality; to say *art-form* is to refer to an individuality. We go from the general to the particular. Somehow, growth or progress in art has to do with the enhancement of given individual characteristics in the work of art; and here is where form takes on such importance. To go from the amorphous to the morphological seems to be a fundamental trend in the development of art. We rejoice in the contemplation of an entity, complete in itself, complex in its expression, coherent in all its functions, beautiful in its parts, and harmonious in its ensemble.)Ever since remotest times the human body was revered as a perfect form. Man has ascertained that God created man in his image, because man as an individual (and when I say "man" I mean men and women as a matter of course), man as an anatomic entity, is quite beautiful and perfect. If by "image" we understand physical image, and if man was created in the image of God, God being perfection, man is perfection too. Therefore God, the supreme perfection, and man, at least in his physical appearance according to the biblical decree, are equally beautiful. The oldest documents known—Egyptian, Chinese, Olmec, and so on—speak of the earliest cult of human anatomy, that is, the cult of anthropomorphic gods: the human body was beautiful to their eyes, was beautified and sublimed. Such an approach has not ceased to exist or to be the basic source of the plastic arts, even though today the abstractionists have banned human shape from their creations, as though they were thinking of it constantly but negatively.

Of course man loves his own kind, whatever his kind may be. If the Martians were to seem ugly to us, we would seem just as hideous to them; but they would find each other beautiful.

We must, nevertheless, have other reasons, more or less basic reasons, for loving our own anatomic kind. There is good proportion; there is symmetry; there is a certain amount of homogeneity as well as the required dose of contrast. But why is all this pleasing to us?

Let us not try to explain why. There are many "whys" which we are not able to explain. Why do we like the chords originated by the natural overtones? Why do we like the seven colors of the spectrum? Why is symmetry pleasing? Why do we say an entity is coherent?

There are impossible "whys," questions impossible to answer. We must limit ourselves to acknowledgment of certain facts, regarding them as physical truths, as physical phenomena having a direct relationship to our physical make-up. We humans are part of the universe, ruled by the same over-all laws governing light spectra, acoustical resonance, principles of life, capillarity, osmosis, cyclical phenomena, and the like. There is a primeval kinship between them and us: we must accept that objectively.

We start from the incontestable fact that from the very beginning there were seven natural colors; there were the natural intervals—the octave and the fifth (and so on)—from which a scale called diatonic came to exist; there were rhythm and symmetry in the course of the seasons, the years,[2] the days, the pulse of our hearts, and the growing of all living things. And we love all that. We love it irresistibly.

Rhythm and symmetry—of course—are close concerns to musicians and artists. And though we cannot explain the ultimate causes of their being, we can speculate about their nature.

What is rhythm and what is symmetry?

Both rhythm and symmetry are nothing but certain kinds of repetition: and repetition, this seemingly completely unimportant fact, is not so unimportant; it has had profound consequences in all its human manifestations. Repetition has been from the beginning the driving element of imitation. In imitating, man tried to repeat in one way or another what he saw, and heard, and otherwise noticed around him. Repetition comes directly behind imitation, and imitation—so say the learned authorities—has been the supreme teacher of mankind.

To go directly to our point, repetition has been the decisive factor in giving shape to music and all the fine arts.

If the human body was the model for the first painters and sculptors, it is because the human body already had in itself the organic elements of symmetrical repetition: one arm on one side repeated symmetrically on the other side; two legs in equal symmetrical position; a trunk as a central unit from which both pairs of arms and legs appear symmetrically; a head in singleness, as if it were an element of contrast to make more notable the parity and symmetry. Furthermore, frontally observed, the body is a perfect case of radial symmetry, all the way down from the head to the feet. Man has always received, by his own image, the unequivocal teachings of symmetry and repetition, as well as those evident in nature: the sun rising and setting unfailingly every twenty-four hours, or the ocean waves repeating themselves rhythmically and indefatigably.

Rhyme, one of the basic elements of poematic construction, is nothing but the repetition of a given sound or ending in a symmetrical sequence. Verse, the other essential element, is a grouping of syllables rhythmically disposed. Syllables are the portions subject to rhythmical accentuation, and they correspond to beats in a bar of music, subjected to the same general rules of meter.

Syllables, beats, steps, are all in the same manner the basic structural elements of poetry, music, and dance, respectively, since in the early days these three arts were a single, united practice. Dancing seems at first to have been nothing but a form of walking. It would not be too risky to say that the arts of rhythm—poetry, music, and dance— were born the day man first walked rhythmically. Spontaneous, instinctive walking affords this perfectly symmetrical pattern: $\frac{2}{4}$ $\overset{1}{\downarrow}\ \overset{2}{\downarrow}\ |\ \overset{1}{\downarrow}\ \overset{2}{\downarrow}\ |\ \overset{1}{\downarrow}\ \overset{2}{\downarrow}\ |$ _etc._

As dancing began to develop, other groupings or patterns developed which were called *steps* or *feet,* as coming from walk or dance. These rhythmical portions, or feet, served dancing, poetry, and music equally when the three arts were united in one, and as they later separated, the feet continued to be the basis for the rhythmical structure of each one. Thus steps, or feet, became the very first form-units known: rhythmic cells, conditioned by repetition and symmetry.

As rhyme and verse derive for repetition, so, too, do other poetic expedients: assonance, where repetition is concerned with the sound of vowels; and alliteration, where a less orderly or regimented repetition is of most convincing effect.

In music, repetition as a shaping force is greater than we perhaps think at first sight. The bar consists of repeated beats with accents symmetrically repeated. The forms themselves: A, A, etc., is sheer repetition; A, B, A, is a repetition in bilateral symmetry of A in regard to B; AB, AB, is a symmetrical repetition of the AB group; so is ABC, ABC, etc.; and to make the story short, the sonata, as the peak of classical form, consists of a portion called *exposition* repeated in bilateral symmetry around a central section called *development*.

Exposition
$\begin{cases} \text{A} & \text{Theme A} \\ \text{B} & \text{Theme B} \\ \text{C} & \text{Coda} \end{cases}$

Central section   D   Development

Recapitulation
$\begin{cases} \text{A} & \text{Theme A} \\ \text{B} & \text{Theme B} \\ \text{C} & \text{Coda} \end{cases}$

A rough architectural diagram of this would be as follows:

In music, furthermore, the various devices used to integrate form are, again and again, nothing but methods of repetition. The so-called "development" is a way of repeating, in a fragmentary and diversified manner, the various motives or cells of which the theme is composed. Contrapuntal forms, such as the fugue, canon, and imitation, are obvious modes of repetition. We shall treat this subject in detail in another chapter.

Let us now try to follow the trail of repetition and imitation as originators of art and art-forms.

It seems that Salomon Reinach, more than fifty years ago, was the first to venture a hypothesis on the magic origin of early cave paintings; from this basis Combarieu applied the theory to music and dance.[3]

Magic is a ritual of prehistoric or contemporary primitive men, performed by a magician. The magician is the wise man, a venerated priest who is the authorized depository of the tribal traditions. We understand by primitive, sociologically speaking, the man chronologically anterior to religious cults. The word magician (*mage* in French) designated originally a certain tribe of the Medes, about the sixth century B.C.

The Latin word *incantare* meant to enchant, or enchantment achieved by means of chant. Chant (song) is in itself a power serving the purposes of magic; a very special effect is exercised upon an object, a person, or a spirit.

We can understand magic as a body of practices by means of which man expects to impose his will: that is, magic implies violence. By means of magic formulas man does violence to the invisible spirits that people the earth. This is one instance in which magic and religious cults are essentially opposed. Religious man addresses an omnipotent being, imploring blessing or mercy; the magic man does not pray but commands, as can be gathered by the following words of an incantation by a Papago master magician to bring rain: "Here I am sitting, and with my power I draw the South wind toward me. After the wind, I draw the clouds, and after the clouds I draw the rain that makes the wild flowers grow on our home ground and look so beautiful." [4]

Magic has definite rules and principles, and its rites can be either manual—tracing geometric figures, making images or knots, mixing or burning diverse substances—or oral, mainly in song (Song or chant is the essential of the rite, and manual rites are incomplete without it.)

Magic song does not follow any proper system or musical idea: it obeys the basic principles of imitation and repetition, imitation being understood as a way of likeness acting upon likeness. The principle is simple: the image of a being or object gives its creator or its possessor a power or influence on the being or object itself. It is believed that between the beings and their effigies there is a net of invisible links, so that by altering the latter one can influence the former. This is the key to the prehistoric paintings of animals and later on to the worship of gods in effigy, a universal practice, derived from magic rites, which has not ceased to exist.

Dances, for the same reason, were imitative from their inception. So-called hunting dances are purely mimetic. I remember as a most memorable experience the dance of the deer among the Yaqui Indians of the State of Sonora in Mexico. The Yaquis could not be subdued and remained for centuries in a seminomadic state, completely isolated from Western civilization, living by hunting and primitive agriculture. For the purpose of incantation, in order to seize and dominate the deer, the Yaquis developed one of the most remarkable "dancer's imitations" [5] I have ever known, reproducing the attitudes, movements, and rhythms of this remarkably beautiful animal. The Yaqui is agile, strong, flexible, and extremely sensitive. The dancer wants nothing more nor less than to look like a deer and to do what it does, in the most realistic manner possible. So the man runs wild

for a while, stops suddenly, then walks as it were in slow
motion, moves his head, listens, trying to locate his hunter;
calmly starts over again in the opposite direction. For a
while he feels safe, and confidence gives way to joy; then
again, distrust, caution, a halt; single, scattered nervous
movements—the head, a foot, an arm. Then, toward the end
of the dance, a new character appears: the hunter. There is
the chase, and wild excitement, and death. But even then
the hunter loves the hunted; death is transitory; the deer,
dead or alive, is immortal; the deer is a god.

We know of many dances like this in antiquity and among
contemporary primitives. But there are other kinds of
dances, everyday dances that have survived from the past
and are quite universal. Love dances, for example, are
purely mimetic.

Imitation, however, does not always operate literally, as
in the case of the plastic arts and dancing. There is literal
imitation, and there is also another kind. The ancients said
(poetry is an imitation in the sense that it reproduces certain
states of mind: "When men hear imitations, even apart from
the rhythms and tunes themselves, their feelings move in
sympathy . . . rhythm and melody supply imitations of
anger and gentleness, and also of courage and temperance,
and of all the qualities contrary to these, and of the other
qualities of character, which hardly fall short of the actual
affections, as we know from our own experience, for in listening to such strains our souls undergo a change.")[6]

Poetry and music express states of mind. Thus they have
been, since the beginning, more or less what we now call
expressionism. Sadness or joy, struggle or restraint, vigor
or languor are mirrored by poetry and music, this being a
vast division of ancient lyric and dramatic poetry, as well
as narrative and epic.

In music there are obvious cases of literal imitation, as
when a magic song meant to bring down rain proceeds by

constantly descending intervals. But the greater realm of music has been, ever since the earliest days of incantation, the realm of expressionism in the most natural manner. Sadness made sad music; so did joy, and fear, and violence make their music, and this was a strong weapon against the spirits.∗

It is curious, by the way, how much time it took for the plastic arts to go from literal imitation to expressive imitation. It was not until the advent of Impressionism in the nineteenth century. Before that, the aim of painting and sculpture was to imitate things as "we knew they were," not as we felt them nor as the impression they had left on us. The same could be said of dancing. Gymnastic dance as pure movement, or as beautiful plastic art in movement, is a relatively recent notion.

The whole thing, of course, depends greatly on the nature of the medium; and the very nature of the musical medium, so utterly suitable to take on the shape of our emotions, makes music the ideal instrument of magic.

I have said before that, whereas the religious man implores the favor of God, the primitive magician tries to impose his will on the spirits. It would seem that the most natural and simple expedient to this effect would be a reiterated command, an insistently repeated order. He who has heard the implacable drumming of a magic ritual cannot have the slightest doubt in this regard. This sort of call would be represented by a series of equal beats repeated endlessly in symmetric succession:

Fast: ♩ ♩ ♩ ♩ ♩ ♩ ♩ ♩ *etc.*

[(By repetition we understand and learn;)and only by repetition do we find it possible to make others understand and obey us.]Nature itself also teaches us by repetition. Repetition reigns over all basic phenomena of the physical world, and we imitate nature in its repetitional procedures.

Magic song proceeds by small melodic patterns constantly reiterated. I heard in an Indian festivity in Chalma a dance song that, on a sustained drumming, presented alternately in unlimited repetition an ascending octave and a fifth, linked together by a secondary motive:

Repetition formulas were carried over from incantation to religious rites proper. The Catholic system of prayer is a case in point. A rosary, for instance, is constituted of ten *Hail Marys* and one *Our Father,* repeated five times, plus one *Our Father,* three *Hail Marys,* one *Salve,* and the final litany, where the formula *ora pro nobis* presents itself as an ostinato. We have to prove our devotion to God by repetition, He himself being convinced only by repetition. Evidently the ancient belief that an idea can only be imprinted on the mind by repetition still holds true. Modern propaganda principles confirm it clearly.

The simplest element of repetition, 1–2, could have very well been provided at the beginning by walking. That would be a spondee: ♩♩ | ♩♩ | ♩♩ | *etc.*

or a spondee-anapest: ♩ | ♩♩ | ♩♩ | ♩ *etc.*

I would like to remember that the iambic foot, an early pattern consisting of two strokes of which the first is short and the second long, is in fact a pattern of three. The iamb

was a favorite in ancient times: $\frac{3}{4}$ ♪ ♩ │ ♪ ♩ │ ♪ ♩ │etc.
1 2   1 2   1 2

The same can be said of the trochee:

$\frac{3}{4}$ ♪ │ ♩ ♪ │ ♩ ♪ │ ♩ etc.
1   2   1   2   1   2

Grove says, "The precedence given (in the 12th and 13th centuries) to triple time, *tempus perfectum* (normal) is probably to be explained, not by any fancied ascription to the Trinity, but by the fact that the trochee and iamb, both involving triple time, were the normal metrical feet of poetry, whereas the dactyl and anapest, involving duple time, were abnormal (*imperfectum*)." [8]

One way or the other, the ternary repetitions were one of the most fabulously successful weapons of magic. Three, and three elevated to the square, nine, were the omnipotent occult forces of command. *Ter dico, ter incanto*,[9] they would assert. The rule was to say whatever was said three times, or three times three times.

In any event, whether the triple was older than the duple or not, the ternary foot, the tribrach:

$\frac{3}{4}$ ♪ ♪ ♪ │ ♪ ♪ ♪ │ ♪ ♪ ♪ │ etc.

together with the spondee, provided the foundation for all other rhythmic combinations. All possible rhythmical patterns are clearly nothing but combinations of 2 and 3.

$$
\begin{aligned}
4 &= 2 + 2 \\
5 &= 2 + 3 \\
5 &= 3 + 2 \\
6 &= 2 + 2 + 2
\end{aligned}
\qquad
\begin{aligned}
6 &= 3 + 3 \\
7 &= 2 + 2 + 3 \\
7 &= 2 + 3 + 2 \\
7 &= 3 + 2 + 2, \text{ etc.}
\end{aligned}
$$

We have been dealing with rhythm and symmetry as if we all had a clear concept of them, but I have always thought that these two particular terms are quite pliable and suggest many different notions.

What is rhythm? Much has been said about this, and, without pretending to define it, I would like to make the following observations: rhythm is not an invention of man; it is rather a natural phenomenon with which we are naturally identified. Also, rhythm is an adjective quality. Things either have rhythm or do not have it, as things can be either red or green, or first or second. Such a quality consists of presenting synchronic divisions of time, or equidistant divisions in space. We say that sounds are rhythmical when they are produced at periodic intervals; if the regularity disappears, we say they are not rhythmical. But there is more to it: in order to be rhythmical the synchronic divisions must give a sense of beginning and end. Every certain number of beats constitute a unit. That is to say, every two, every three, every four beats make a rhythmical unit called a bar or a measure. This is achieved by the prosodic accentuation falling on the first beat (thesis) and a certain weakness on the last (arsis).

Summing up: rhythm is an adjective quality of a series of a) equal divisions in time or space, b) having prosodic accents at equal distances.

Symmetry is an adjective quality implying a) the existence in time or space of two or more equal or identical elements, b) placed at equal intervals or distances. Symmetry is also necessarily referred to as a given composition of elements that can be placed at different relative positions.

Anthropologists have given us some very good hints on this matter;[10] I would like to present a more definite scheme (page 48).

The same thing applied to design is contained in the little drawings on page 49, and applied to music, in the examples beneath the drawings.

Rhythm and symmetry are the essentials of musical construction. Rhythmical and symmetrical repetition operate as the basic and universal principle for rudimentary as well

Bilateral Symmetry

```
A|A              A              A|A        A A
AB|AB     or     ─        A|B   A|B        B B
ABC|ABC          A        A|A              C C
                          B|B              ─────
                                           A A
                                           B B
                                           C C
```

Radial Symmetry or Mirror

```
AB|BA            A              A          A
ABC|CBA   or     B              B          B
ABCD|DCBA        ─        A|B   C          C
                 B              ─          D
                 A              C          ─
                                B          D
                                A          C
                                           B
                                           A
```

Inverted Symmetry

```
A        A        A               ABC
B C      B D      B E      or     ───
C B      C C      C D             CBA
A        D B      D C
         A        E B
                  A
```

Doubly Inverted Symmetry

```
A        A        A               ABC
B Ɔ      B ᗡ      B Ǝ      or     ───
C ᗺ      C Ɔ      C ᗡ             ∀BƆ
∀        D ᗺ      D Ɔ
         ∀        E ᗺ
                  ∀
```

BILATERAL SYMMETRY

1   2
Head Up   Head Up
Back Left   Back Left

RADIAL SYMMETRY OR MIRROR

1   2
Head Up   Head Up
Back Left   Back Right

INVERTED SYMMETRY

1   2
Head Up   Head Down
Back Left   Back Left

DOUBLY INVERTED SYMMETRY

1   2
Head Up   Head Down
Back Left   Back Right

Bilateral Symmetry

Radial Symmetry or Mirror

Inverted Symmetry

Doubly Inverted Symmetry

as larger structures. The same rhythmic principles that operate to integrate one bar operate to integrate phrases, sections, parts, or a whole piece of music.

As I said before, themes or parts are balanced in composition according to symmetrical disposition. It goes without saying that musical forms in our day are more elaborate and developed than in the early days, but they remain essentially A, A, A, etc., AB, AC, AD, etc., ABC, ABC, etc.; that is to say, *prototype* forms became *archetype* forms: ballade, rondo, sonata, etc. They remained basically the same because for centuries they proved to be satisfactory and efficacious. So, sonnet and sonata are form-structures of definite shape that time has consecrated and nobody would contest. They have followed a natural logic and have ended by establishing a formalistic logic. We are instinctively convinced of that logic, to the point that archetype forms are for us beautiful in themselves. (That is why they are archetypes.)

However, artistic creation is dynamic by nature, a force permanently acting against the general rule, the archetype form, and traditional logic. There have also been the surrealists. "We still live in the realm of logic," they say. [11] The "rights to liberty" would come from the liberation of logic and consciousness. The dream and automatisms of the unconscious would be the promised land.

The emancipation of conscious thought, the emancipation of logic, implies the emancipation of archetype forms and academic logic. That would be quite an experience! But music has not had much to do with surrealism—in fact, nothing to do with surrealism, as if music and surrealism were declared enemies. That is too bad. When are musicians going to write music without premeditation? Musicians, I mean musician-composers, preach logic, intelligent order, conscious organization. How close or far are musicians from the "psychic automatism" that would "dictate in absence of any and all control exercised by reason outside of all and every ethic or esthetic preoccupation"?

The superior reality of music is something to be considered in what for us, trained and incurable logicians, would be the realm of the arbitrary. The more arbitrary, the clearer. There is, however, in music a surrealistic atmosphere per se (depending on the music, of course); a sort of superior breathing air as though it bestowed life in high-up, left-hand, right-hand levels. How we can make a conjugation of realities down below and up above without being stripped of our traditional garments is something to be only dimly imagined.

One cannot conceive surrealism's acknowledging the validity of any archetype whatever, nor of anything else that could interfere with the free play of the subconscious. Nevertheless, we have already been aware of the conscious and unconscious parts of the creative process in music, as if, at least theoretically, creation were subconscious and composition the conscious putting in order and organizing of the work.

In any case, the matter gets more and more involved when the possibility appears that we cannot very well determine just how free automatic thinking can be. Is our automatic thinking really free? Can it be free?

It is most probable that the subconscious is imbued with logic. This is a sad realization. Atavism has rooted symmetric rhythmical patterns very deeply in our subconscious. Automatism will therefore obey atavistic logic. If that is the case, what hope can we still have in surrealism? Very likely music is one of the most, or the most, ductile of all artistic media to express the depths of the subconscious. It would be necessary to dispose of deep-rooted atavisms, to clean out our minds in order to permit unbiased thought. We should have to remove, somehow, the shadows of a rigid past falling upon us.

However, I am not committing myself at all to a possible "surrealistic" music. We do not merely want to exchange an academic label for a surrealistic one, as seems to have happened with a good deal of surrealistic painting and sculpture. We shall have the opportunity in a future chapter to come back to the possibility of an unforeseen, unpremeditated music. Nevertheless, the old teachings still hold good for us today in the matter of coherence and the integration of a unity—that is to say, form. How much has been achieved by the surrealists in this direction is still to be proven, not by us but by time. In any event, we can still say that we want a work of art to be a unit, "a complete whole in itself, with a beginning, a middle, and an end, so as to enable the work to produce its own proper pleasure, with all the organic unity of a living creature." [12] And we still understand a whole as that "which has beginning, middle, and end. A beginning is that which is not itself necessarily after anything else, and which has naturally something else after it; an end is that which is naturally after something itself, either as its necessary or usual consequent, and with nothing else after it; and a middle, that which is by nature after one thing and has also another after it." [13]

A unit, then, must have parts that are functional, that is, specifically fitted to open and close, and united by a section especially fitted to link both. A whole in which each part fulfills a specific function as in the case of a living organism—this concept could not be clearer, more universal, or more lasting. But by definition a "living creature" is not static: it moves forward, undergoes constant and eternal changes.

Within the last twenty centuries of musical history there has been considerable development toward more coherent forms. From the early plain song and secular songs to the counterpoint of *Ars Nova* was quite a step, as it was from there to the symphonies of the eighteenth century, and again to those of the nineteenth century. What a stretch was covered by the man who composed that miracle of form which is called *La Mer*—and what a stretch from this to the neatly organized Webernian miniatures!

There has also been progress in that in modern times large forms have been possible in music. Actual dimension or bigness is not the main point; but it takes a greater greatness to conceive the major forms of Beethoven's Ninth or Debussy's *La Mer*. Here again the idea is not new: "To be beautiful, a living creature, and every whole made up of parts, must not only present a certain order in its arrangements of parts, but also be of a certain definite magnitude. Beauty is a matter of size and order . . ." [14]

"A matter of size . . . A certain definite magnitude." Let us beware of the grandiose for the sake of the "bigger and better"; but let us remember that actual size has a lot to do with the problems of form (although miniaturists, of course, would disagree). Actual size, proportionate to our physical capacity for sustained attention and grasp of the ensemble, is a relationship in constant evolution, and for that reason difficult to ascertain. But, somehow, smallness of form is linked to the idea of minority of age. It would be difficult to say why. Nevertheless, coherence being the desideratum, large forms are more apt to be incoherent, and the accomplishment of an *Eroica* still leaves us in wonderment.

We have seen how music and the other arts have depended on the basic factors of repetition and imitation. To what extent have these expedients been successful in achieving unity of form, cohesion in music?

All in all, by these procedures the classic ideals of form have been wonderfully fulfilled, and every historical period has offered an array of solutions. However, one wonders how long-lived and how diversely disguised repetition will have to be in days to come—or will there be other possibilities? To what degree is repetition, so connatural to us, actually to our pleasure? And to what extent, no matter how concealed, will repetition end by fatiguing us?

One should conclude with a conclusion instead of finishing with a question, but this question provides a topic for discussion in the following chapter.

IV

Repetition in Music

We may perhaps say that, from the standpoint of form and construction, a piece of music is not a solid block but an aggregate of parts that constitute a unity. The intrinsic value of each part and the degree of cohesion existing between all the parts are the ultimate measure of the actual merit or artistic value of the piece.

But there are parts; parts which compose the whole, and parts which compose the parts, and parts which compose the parts of the parts, and so forth and so on. There are parts of differing sizes and varied importance and meaning: a well-graded hierarchy of parts which begins with the smallest group of notes that makes sense by itself and ends with a large architectural unit. The smallest group of notes is called the *motive* and should consist of two or more notes. The motive has a rhythmical pattern on the same or differ-

55

ent melodic intervals. Anybody can remember the remarkable two-note motive of Beethoven's Ninth Symphony of which the rhythmical pattern is

♪ | ♩

on intervals alternating fifths and fourths.

It is my desire to consider in the following paragraphs to what extent repetition is an underlying principle in musical construction, and then proceed to illustrate the point objectively.

Let us take the first sixteen bars of the first movement of the symphony already mentioned, which constitute a small introduction to the main theme. The second violins and cellos have a pedal, a sextuplet on A, repeated all the way through; that is to say, sixteen repeated bars. In the upper part, the first phrase (four bars) is made up of the two-note motive appearing symmetrically repeated:

♪ | ♩ ₇·· ♪ | ♩ ₇·· ♪ | ♩

To be specific, by "symmetrical" I mean a group of two identical or very similar elements placed at both sides of, and at an equal distance from, a real or imaginary axis, which constitutes bilateral symmetry.

The second phrase (four bars) repeats the previous four in bilateral symmetry:

       I   II

♪ | ♩ ₇·· ♪ | ♩ ₇·· ♪ | ♩ 𝄽 | 𝄾 ₇·· ♪ | ♩ ₇·· ♪ | ♩ ₇·· ♪ | ♩

The next six bars corroborate the foregoing: the phrase is constructed by means of repetition of

(I) the two-note motive at shorter distances (always symmetrical);

(II) repetition of the same intervals—fourths and fifths
—in a different rhythmical pattern; and

(III) repetition of the same rhythmical pattern (sixteenths) in repeated octaves:

The introduction leads directly into the main theme,
which is a period consisting of eighteen bars, the first two
bars presenting the definitive manner of the two-note motive, that is, a repetition of it over a D minor chord in the
range of two octaves:

These first two bars, containing the most important part
of the main subject—the head of the theme—are, then,
nothing but a repetition of the two-note motive, reiterated
in such a way as to acquire a remarkable character of its
own.

The remaining fourteen bars present new material which
we are not going to discuss at the moment.

We shall now look at a *section,* the one meant to expose
the main theme, consisting of

(I) the introduction; and

(II) the main theme, both of which the composer proceeds to repeat right away. The structure, in four
parts, would be represented as follows:

Section

Period I: 16 bars	Period III: 16 bars
Introduction in A	Introduction in D
Period II: 18 bars	Period IV: 12 bars
Main theme in d	Main theme in B♭

We see, then, that the section consists of four periods, III and IV being a repetition of I and II. That is to say, instead of I, II, III, IV, the section is built of I and II and the recurrence of I and II, two blocks entirely alike disposed in bilateral symmetry.

For the sake of clarity we had better call things by their names. I have already mentioned periods and sections. Let us agree on the matter of names. A piece of music is made up of parts of different sizes, as I said. Let us give names to these parts, according to their lengths, and establish their relative positions. The length varies, of course, according to the scope of the piece, but we can safely say that a group of *bars* makes a *phrase;* a group of phrases makes a *period;* a group of periods makes a *section;* a group of sections makes a *part;* and a group of parts makes a *piece* of music (or technically, a *song*). To complete the picture: since music is an art developing in time, it has to be structured and measured in time. The various units that constitute that structure, and their relative lengths, are, from the smallest to the largest, more or less like this:

Beat	is the unit of time-measure
Bar	=1, 2, 3, etc., beats
Phrase	= 2, (3),* or 4 bars

* The tripartite construction of phrases, periods, and sections is very rare in classical music.

Period   = 2, (3), or 4 phrases
Section = 2, (3), or 4 periods
Part   = 2, 3, or 4 sections
Piece (song) = 2, 3, or 4 parts

This is only a general scheme, meant to facilitate our discussion. It shows, however, in an objective way that the measure is a repetition of equal beats symmetrically accented (that is, every two, three, or four, etc., beats); a phrase is a repetition of bars equal in length; and, similarly, a period a repetition of phrases, a section a repetition of periods, and so on.

Now, it is common knowledge that repetition in various guises is a procedure in the development of themes. But outright repetition procedures often serve also to integrate a theme proper. Let us take the second theme of the same symphony, a phrase of four bars, and the little bridge theme that precedes it. The latter consists of the element:

repeated three times in a stepwise sequence (dominant, tonic, dominant):

the second theme consists of a motive of two notes:

repeated four times in rhythmical sequence.

I should like to mention in passing that perhaps it would be better to look at this as a three-note motive with elision:

		Number of Bars	4-Note Motive	Total
PART I (Exposition)	Introduction Bars 1–5	5	2 times	
	Main theme Bars 6–58	53	43 times	
	Bridge Bars 59–62	4	1 time	
	Second theme Bars 63–109	47	10 times	
	Coda Bars 110–124	15	10 times	66 66 times
PART II (Development)	Bars 125–247	123	59 times	59 125 times
PART III (Recapitulation)	Introduction Bars 248–252	5	2 times	
	Main theme Bars 253–302	50	42 times	
	Bridge Bars 303–306	4	1 time	
	Second theme Bars 307–361	55	11 times	
	Coda Bars 362–373	12	10 times	66 191 times
PART IV (Second development)	Bars 374–502	129	39 times	39 230 times*

* The repetition of the exposition is not taken into account here.

There is a conspicuous case where the motivic construction is carried to an extreme, and an almost literal repetition is the principle by which a whole movement of a symphony takes shape. It is of course hardly necessary to mention that I refer to the *Allegro con brio* of the Fifth Symphony, where the immeasurable genius of Beethoven performed a miracle which still keeps the world in amazement. Affecting various intervals:

the rhythmical pattern of four notes is the universal element in the various parts of the allegro, appearing 230 times, filling 298 measures out of 502, three fifths of the whole musical matter of the piece. (See page 60.)

It is to be remarked that the four-note motive is not only the main element of the first theme, but also appears integrated in the bridge theme:

and interwoven in the second theme:

Repetition, again, worked out to integrate the other themes of this allegro in more ways than the usual: the bridge, an admirable, concise theme, consists of two fifths in succession, tonic and dominant:

The second theme is a melody formed by two ascending intervals, fourth and second, repeated descending, fourth and second:

These four bars, which constitute the first phrase, or antecedent of the period, are stated three consecutive times, bars 63–74; a considerable reiteration to make up for the lack of consequent proper.

The pattern of the sequence that follows immediately after is constructed of seconds, one ascending, one descending, in bars 1 and 2, repeated in bars 3 and 4 in bilateral symmetry:

The ensuing development of this element proceeds in a sequential progression. Coming directly from polyphony, sequences are one of the most favored constructional devices. Sequences, of course, are repetitions or series of repetitions of either a melodic or a rhythmical pattern, or of both, stepwise or otherwise. Sequences serve all purposes, but they are especially suited for developments.

I should like to continue quoting Beethoven as the undisputed, universal master, whose influence is felt even by the most advanced masters of our day.

In the first allegro of the Pastoral Symphony (bars 151–236), there is a five-note pattern repeated in sequence thirty-six consecutive times; then, the first two notes of the pattern, eight times; then, after a little bridge of six bars, the whole thing—forty bars—is repeated:

Such composition would provide the following scheme:

40 bars (repeated in sequence)	6 bars	40 bars (repeated in sequence)

This bilateral symmetry seems to be very necessary for our sense of balance. We need symmetrical dispositions at any moment, in any part, large or small, and do not seem to be happy without it. If something stands here, we need the same sort of thing repeated there, side by side.

We have seen before how phrases, periods, sections, are symmetrical within themselves. The whole piece (or *song*), of course, is also symmetrical. The grand coda in the allegros of Beethoven's symphonies takes the place of a true second development; and this is a fact worth examining in relation to the quest for strict symmetry in the structure of the whole piece (or *song*). The sonata form in symphonies traditionally consists of:

   (I) Exposition
  (II) Development
 (III) Recapitulation

However, a scheme of the structure of the Fifth Symphony, to cite one case, presents the following:

(I) Exposition
(II) Development
(III) Recapitulation
(IV) Second development

There are, then, four parts instead of three: four parts of exactly the same weight, the third and fourth a recurrence of the first and second, each one of the parts having 125 bars, 4 × 125 making a total of 500. To be exact, the number of measures is 502, and the parts have 124, 123, 126, and 129 respectively. This could not possibly be accidental. It is quite clear that Beethoven wished the exposition and development to be balanced by a recapitulation and a second development of exactly the same importance, two blocks of rigorously bilateral symmetry:

Whole piece (or *song*)

Exposition 124 bars	Recapitulation 126 bars
Development I 123 bars	Development II 129 bars

Instances where the theme itself is nothing but an aggregation of identical molecules are innumerable, and much more frequent than it would appear at first sight. I should like to recall the case of the first movement of the First Symphony of Beethoven.

Three notes miraculously give the theme a very definite physiognomy because they are repeated in a certain way.

Indeed, the miracle is not performed by repetition itself
but by the genius of the composer, that is to say, by the
way the repetition is managed:

Three notes are repeated five times—this is the antecedent; it does not seem to have any consequent, at least immediately, for before anything else happens, the motive,
covering by consecutive repetition the four bars of the
phrase, is repeated twice more in sequences hardly bridged
by two chords. So the actual statement of the theme consists in the presentation of one phrase three times, the first
two phrases containing the motive five times, and the last
seven:

In a period of eighteen bars the little motive appears
repeated seventeen times. The first phrase of the second
theme does not consist of a motive repeated outright—as it
does in the first theme—but of a four-note motive repeated
four times in sequence. The theme itself is a sequence on
the tonic, subtonic, dominant, and tonic again:

Almost everything—themes, phrases, periods, little bridges, etc.—is said twice, or four times; seldom three times, but almost never once. Even themes proper—periods of two phrases—are very often built in what is called *parallel construction,* which is a repetition of the given phrase with a different cadence.

This composition by pairs provides great comfort to the listener. Somehow, music that is rich in repetition is also rich in success—although it should be clearly understood that I am not proclaiming that repetition is its only condition.

I would like to recall a semiclassical, semipopular song of very great appeal, Gershwin's "It Ain't Necessarily So," where the basic motive consists of three notes separated by an ascending and a descending interval, followed immediately by the same pattern changing the fifth to a fourth, and then by the same pattern incomplete, that is, only the ascending interval, a third:

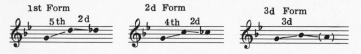

The three forms of the element, put together, constitute the antecedent of the theme and go like this:

This is repeated, or stated twice, to complete the antecedent phrase; and the second phrase, or consequent, uses the first form of the motive once, followed immediately by the third form of the motive repeated six times:

A short melodic turn, to make the cadence, is the same motive followed by a descending third in inverted symmetry:

Plain song aside, it is a fact that all music, of all times, has always followed a given meter, whether it is the same from the beginning to the end, or has more or less successive changes of time-signature. Frequent changes of time-signature within the same piece occur in music of very recent date, and this fact we will consider later. But we can say that, before the twentieth-century composers, and all the way back to Greece, music has been based on a uniform meter throughout a given piece.

Greek music was essentially based on dance and poetry, and to that extent it was also based on metric feet. Certainly from the Greeks on, dance music through the centuries has obviously followed time-measure.

The Greek feet and the modern time-measure are not essentially different: the former we may define as a fixed rhythmical pattern provided with an accented beat. The fundamental element of strong (thesis) and weak (arsis) beats was present. A Greek foot was a given time-measure with a given, unchanged rhythmical pattern; ours is a time-measure of fixed, unchanged beats, where we freely put in all sorts of rhythmical patterns.

But dance music with which we are familiar nowadays, that is, dance music of the last three or four hundred years, keeps the Greek foot, or naked rhythmical pattern, in the "accompaniment" or lower parts, as is obvious in a waltz. *Tribrach* (♪♪♪) or *mollosos* (♩♩♩) is the likeliest ancestor of the waltz:

A simple *pyrrhic* (♪♪) or a *spondee* (♩♩) could be the earliest ancestor of the march; a *dispondee* (♩♩♩♩) is very likely a nearer ancestor:

And of course the *hexabrachys* is nothing but the present:

⁶₈ ♫♫ ♫♫ | ♫♫ ♫♫ | *etc.*

which has met with so much favor among folk dances of many countries.

Even the *habanera* might be traced back to a combination of an amphibrach (♪♩♪) and a *spondee* (♩♩), the two combined being: ♪♩ ♪♩ ♩ or ♫♩♫

But be the accompaniment a simple obbligato or one of the more elaborate shapes later found in the homophonic forms perfected by Haydn, Mozart, Beethoven, etc., the principle at which I am driving is that music rests on the fundamental principle of the beat, which is synchronic and symmetrically accented. In this sense, an *alla breve* Mozart allegro with clearly marked beats differs little from a most primitive musical incantation accompanied by a constant steady drumming: a compelling, powerful, hypnotic effect of repeated beats obstinately maintained.

There is, for example, the sort of *moto perpetuo* so dear to the great masters of the eighteenth and nineteenth centuries, as much as to the motorized masters of the twentieth, where the motion goes on and on for many bars like this:

ta ca ta ca ta ca ta ca　ta ca ta ca ta ca ta ca　ta ca ta ca ta ca ta ca

Or else:

Beethoven, IV Symphony, FINALE

A pattern formed of notes of the same value is a most common manner of repetition having tremendous appeal. This figuration on even notes is, of course, not confined to sixteenth notes. Series of quarter notes, or eighth notes, during whole phrases or periods, establish a constant symmetry of a very comfortable nature:

Beethoven, I Sonata for Piano

This steady pattern may change for a little while, only to give way to a recurrence which is then doubly satisfying.

The terrific appeal of repetition, and its pleasing, or driving, or hypnotic, or exciting values, have been understood and carried to an extreme by one of the greatest masters of the twentieth century, a high priest, a great master magician of repetition: the composer of *Petrouchka* and *Threni*.

He has proceeded in a way that we may call repetition by accumulation, or accumulated repetition, this being the principle of composition in the melodic elements proper as well as the contrapuntal complexion of the piece. Such procedures start with *Petrouchka* and *Le Sacre du Printemps*, and are never to be abandoned.

It is hardly necessary to recall the type of repetitive, primitive melody that Stravinsky made so popular in the world of occidental music, but I should mention the following typical cases:

PETROUCHKA, Danse Russe

LE SACRE DU PRINTEMPS, Introduction

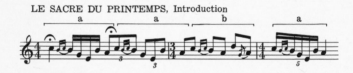

For another example, this time of the contrapuntal element, let us take his "Danse de la Terre," from *Le Sacre du Printemps*. We find the following: a piece of music fifty-eight bars long (plus two bars introduction); an ostinato bass in sixteenth notes covering the whole fifty-eight bars in a two-bar pattern of which the first bar is repeated separately as follows:

Then, beginning in the tenth bar, a new motive in triplets is initiated and presents itself fully in bar 23, to continue without interruption until the end. This is again a simple four-note motive insisting incessantly on a) a fourth, b) the repetition of the lower note, and c) the four notes in descending scale:

These three elements are shuffled constantly, and each is indifferently repeated as follows:

and finally, beginning on bar 29 and going through without interruption until six bars before the end, a last motive in ostinato sixteenths presents itself:

preceded and followed by a chord repeated at different intervals during the first twenty-two and the last six bars:

The last D major chord is superimposed on a reiterated four-note motive in stepwise thirds as follows:

In short, the whole thing is a superimposition of four different ostinatos: one in the bass, another in the middle, one more in the upper part, the fourth being the timpani playing in a truly primitive way uninterrupted sixteenths during fifty-two out of the fifty-eight bars—a sort of apotheosis of the ostinato:

I am not going to discuss here the supreme art with which this is done. I am simply trying to illustrate the repetitional structure devised by this colossal inventor.

There can be no doubt that this composer made a conscious principle out of repetitional construction, although we do not know much from him to that effect. Indeed, we open any page of *Le Sacre* or *Les Noces* and it is perfectly obvious. The same is true of all his music, in a greater or lesser degree, including his very recent compositions.

It is interesting that in *Threni* (1958) we find the master following very much the same repetitional procedures of *Le Sacre:* long harmonic pedals, ostinato melodies, a superimposition of ostinato melodies.

I shall take *De Elegia Prima* (page 4 of the full score); the basic shape and its derivates are as follows:

Bars 19–22: exposition of series A.

Bars 23–26: exposition of series B'.

Bars 27–32: a pedal using notes 11–12 of B' with the chorus *parlando*.

Bars 33–34: exposition of series B.

Bars 35–41: a pedal using notes 10–11–12 of series B, chorus *parlando*.

Bars 42–61: Coro (Soprani-Alti) sings an ostinato melody on series A'. Repetition proceeds in the following manner:

```
             1 2 3 4 5
             1 2 3 4 5 6 7
                 4 5 6 7 8 9 10
                       8 9
                       8 9 10 11 12
                            12
                            12
                            12
                            12
                            12
                            12
                            12
                            12
                            12
        1 2
           2 3 4 5 6 7 8 9 10 11 12
                            12   twenty-one times
```

The same thing in musical notation would be as follows:

Superimposed on the previous choral part, Tenor I (Solo) sings an ostinato melody on series C:

```
1 2 3 4 5
1 2 3 4 5 6 7 8
1 2 3 4 5 6 7 8
            7 8 9 10 11 12
        5 6 7 8 9 10 11 12
1 2 3 4 5 6 7 8 9 10 11 12
```

A third ostinato melody is given to the Bugle C-alto on

the same series C (by diminution) while the previous two
melodies go on. It goes as follows:

```
1 2 3 4 5 6
          5 6 7 8 9 10 11 12
1 2 3 4 5
        4 5 6 7 8 9 10 11 12
1 2 3 4 5
        4 5 6 7 8 9 10
                      9 10 11 12
1 2 3 4 5 6 7 8 9 10 11 12
1 2 3 4 5 6 7 8 9 10 11 12
```

Finally, a fourth element, a melody on a series of three
notes, C, D, F, given to Violins I and II and Violas, goes
on at the same time, the ostinato pattern composed as follows, 1 being C, 2 being D, and 3 being F:

```
1 - 1 - 1 - 2 - 2 - 1 - 1 - 1 - 2 - 1 - 1 - 2 -
1 - 2 - 2 - 3 - 3 - 3 - 2 - 3 - 2 - 1 - 1 - 2 -
1 - 2 - 2 - 2 - 3 - 3 - 2 - 3 - 3 - 3 - 2 - 2 -
1 - 2 - 1 - 2 - 2 - 3 - 2 - 1 - 2 - 1 - 2 - 1 -
2 - 3 - 3 - 2 - 2 - 3 - 2 - 2 - 1 - 2 - 3 - 2 - 3 -
```

Summing up, the ensemble of ostinato melodies proceeds
in the following manner:

Now this section, comprising the pedals to the chorus *parlando* and the counterpoint of ostinato melodies as described before, going from bar 27 to bar 61, is later on repeated twice, from bar 76 to bar 107, and from bar 123 to bar 162, where *De Elegia Prima* ends. Both repetitions undergo only minor adjustments to fit different texts.

There is no question that in *Le Sacre* the composer wanted and had to be primitive, since straightforward repetition is the fundamental element in "primitiveness." We are apt to think, probably for no reason at all, that a good Russian can always be a good primitive and properly deal with *La Russie Païenne,* incantation formulas, and commanding repetitions. But, on the other hand, when Stravinsky came to Paris in 1910 with the score of *The Fire Bird* under his arm, musically he had not gone much beyond Rimsky-Korsakov's rhetorical orientalism, and it was then that he first met the more sophisticated Parisian groups. Satie and the French Impressionists had achieved remarkable things since the 1880's and 90's in harmonic pedals and all sorts of ostinato formulas. Hardly three years after his first direct contact with Paris, Stravinsky returned there with *Le Sacre* and proved to be *plus papiste que le Pape* in the matter of pedals and ostinatos. He has subsequently continued to explore these possibilities, as all his music shows, including the latest. I happen to know, however, of only one instance when he referred to the subject

of repetition, in a story that Lincoln Kirstein tells in his
recent essay, "What Ballet is About." He says: "When
Balanchine was making *Jeux de Cartes* (1937) he found an
ingenious device in which the pack unfolded itself in fan-
like conformations, from the suite King, Queen, Jack, etc.,
held in a poker hand. He made the dancers vary the
sequence three times, each totally different. Stravinsky,
with the parsimony of experience, told him simply to repeat
the first one unchanged three times: 'They won't see it the
first, nor applaud till the third.'" [1] That is to say: the audience does not see it the first time; the audience needs
repeated opportunities to see or hear it.

Indeed, this is one of the points of the philosophy behind
the whole matter: repetition is a way of making oneself
understood quickly and unmistakably, as in incantation.

There is a second point. To achieve unity of form has
been a supreme aim of all eras. Repetition has been the expedient employed to achieve unity with just enough variety,
an answer to the old and endless discussion of unity and
variety, or similarity and contrast, or order and chaos. The
various devices of musical composition have made possible
a thematic treatment and a thematic structure, both based
on repetition, which have so far been believed to guarantee
unity without monotony.

There is also a third point. Repetition is the condition of
symmetry. We instinctively enjoy symmetric dispositions;
we are the owners of symmetric bodies; we are used to
thinking in terms of bilateral symmetry—two sides, right
and left, or two heights, up and down. Repetition and symmetry are thus a matter of good balance and proportion in
the interplay of elements and are thus the essential condi-
tions to integrated form.

If we consider the first point, repetition as a commanding and convincing procedure, we can be either pessimistic
or optimistic about audiences. So far our great classical
masters do not seem to have been terribly optimistic. They

thought they had to state, restate, and corroborate in order to be understood, in order to be clear. This poses a basic problem of relationship between composer and audience: how intelligent and receptive does the composer suppose his audience to be? We have already speculated in previous chapters on the incentives of artistic creation, and it seems that a creative artist proceeds both from an urge to communicate and as a result of the desire to project himself. Does he then choose to communicate with his equals—his equals of today or tomorrow—or does he prefer to speak to his juniors? That remains a consideration for the composer and a decision for him to make.

The second point pronounces repetition as the chief expedient in the drive for unity. It is true that repetition achieves unity in the same sense that nothing resembles a table more than the table itself. To what extent is this unity, and to what extent comfort? Repetition is agreeable and comfortable, and the more repetition, the less effort required of our memory and other receptive capacities. Repetition has the power to turn new acquaintances into old; and how soon this is achieved depends on the degree of passivity of the second person. If we sharpen our receptive capacities, if we improve our memory, if curiosity increases, if our initiative does not decay, we depend less and less on repetition. No matter how disguised the artifices of composition may be (variation, reverse and retrograde, expansion, partitioning, sequence, etc.), repetition will always remain repetition. In fact the question of *repetition* or *newness* resolves itself into an equation of initiative of the listener and newness of the music, as opposed to passivity of the listener and repetitiousness of the music, an equation whose terms vary with the condition of the individual and the nature of the music. In other words, the more apt we are to appreciate new things, the sooner we will tire of repetition.

Now, about the third point. We like symmetry for its own

sake, simply because it is beautiful in itself. We are not sure, however, that we might not like other dispositions, asymmetrical or nonsymmetrical, which would determine new concepts of form, new principles of balance and proportion in matters of composition. We are not sure that our inclination for symmetry is innate and not necessarily a matter of custom and tradition. The history of man's endeavors is a history of experimentation. Nothing is certain, nothing is definite. Creative men are always experimenting; when they succeed we call their experiment a masterpiece; when they do not succeed, we do not even hear of it. A true work of art is nothing but a successful experiment.

General musical taste and the esthetic approach to music has undergone enormous expansion since the days of Haydn. The last two hundred years have seen a tremendous evolution in music: harmony, polytonality, and atonality; developments in the whole sense of musical sonority; rhythmic expansion, both in the liberty with which rhythmical patterns take shape and in the freedom to change meters in the course of a piece, as well as in the wide use of polyrhythms.

These advances in the rhythmical complexion of music express in themselves a considerable reaction against the steadiness of meter and the regularity of rhythmical patterns, or against outright repetition and symmetry as practiced by the masters of two hundred years ago: it can be seen in the rhythmical complexion of Copland's Symphony No. 2 as compared with that of a Mozart allegro. But the traditional constructional procedures, based on repetition and symmetry, remain in force both for polyphonic and homophonic music, with no important or substantial changes. We have seen how Stravinsky relies on some sort of primitive ostinato and repetitional construction, which, however, do not exclude the traditional devices. Schoenberg's principles of musical form do not differ in the least from the polyphonic and homophonic traditional procedures: sequences, imitations, canons, inversions of various sorts, transpositions, disposition of phrases, periods, sections, and parts. That is to say, all the constructional devices based on repetition and symmetry as practiced by the great classical composers are present.

In fact, classical music established a trend of thematic economy that has not changed in the mind of composers. So they stick to the classic procedures to achieve it, taking no chances in a matter which is of paramount importance.

Some few indications, however, can be found here or there in the other direction, and I should like to mention one I consider of real significance.

In his first eight symphonies Beethoven adhered in the strictest way to the principles of thematic economy. (I am referring concretely to the initial allegros.) Suddenly, in the Ninth, he does not seem to be afraid to depart a little from the very tight principles he had set for himself in this respect. In the course of the whole piece—the initial allegro of the Ninth Symphony—there are a number of motives of remarkable individuality that notwithstanding fulfill only the function of little bridges or unimportant episodes. Most remarkable, the main theme is a long one, with an amazing span of eighteen bars; one of continuous melodic expression, containing in itself at least some fourteen motives:

There is certainly a big difference between the frugal four-note motive of the Fifth and this generous theme eighteen bars long, containing so many motives, some of them never developed.

Then, of course, another proof of a bit more confidence in memory was given by Schoenberg, in spite of his very traditional position, in the requirements he established for the "basic shape" (*grundgestalt*): no note is to be repeated before the other eleven have appeared.

As a listener I sometimes find myself thoroughly disinclined to go on listening to repetitious music. It soon begins to become obvious; I remember it too well; and I would prefer to impose a little more effort on my memory. This does not mean that my interest in repetitious music is finished forever. It simply means that I have to give my memory time to forget, and after some months, or years, according to the case, I listen to repetitious music with a renewed interest. Also, I think, we are lucky to be able to like things for what they are, and not necessarily for what we would like them to be: we like Beethoven as Beethoven, and Schoenberg as Schoenberg. It is also true that we, as listeners, have considerable adaptability or, shall I say, a very wide range of possibilities for esthetic enjoyment; which means that, for instance, our pleasure in enjoying polytonal or atonal music does not do away with our capacity to enjoy tonal music.

But perhaps by reason of that very amplitude of range we cannot stand still. It would not be easy to maintain that repetition, with all its various devices, is forever going to be the only way to achieve unity in musical composition.

As a practical consideration, the question now arises of how radical a departure from repetition we may expect in the future. There are, of course, many sides to this matter. It is quite clear that music based on repetitional patterns has a quick and strong impact: it is easy to follow and it is

agreeable to our natural or traditional symmetrical dispositions. But if we soon learn to like repetitious music, on further acquaintance we also soon begin to find repetition
more or less obvious and eventually more or less monoto-
nous. We rejoice in agreeable, easygoing experiences, but
this is not all we are looking for. We would just as soon look
for the new and unexpected, according to our degree of
initiative.

In our mental and spiritual life we are subject to a constant interplay of passive and active forces. We like quie-
tude, rest, easiness, on the ground of our passive leanings,
and for that matter we like comfortable, repetitional patterns; but we also like, and need and strive for, the new and
the unknown, as the incurable seekers of new truths we
naturally are. Our preference for repetition or for newness
may be a matter of individual predilection: some of us may
have more or less passivity. But in the long run we all move
forward and cannot forever remain passive or negative. Life
is, after all, positive. In every process of our intellect and
spirit—in thinking, reacting to art expressions, or the like—
the two main elements are lazy memory (which corresponds
to the passive) and keen expectation (which corresponds to
the active). Lazy memory implies the need for repetition,
and in that sense it is a passive element; expectation comes
from what we do not know but want to know, and in that
sense it is the active element in our endeavors. Forgetfulness and expectation, or rest and curiosity, are the terms of
such a contradiction.

There is also a time element to consider. Repetition fills
the needs of a rather passive life, where time is of little
moment; curiosity enhances the value of time, which moves
by faster and acquires enormous significance. When the
whole process of life becomes intensified time becomes
shorter: the value of time is relative to our rhythm of life,
and our rhythm of life is relative to the degree of pressure
exercised by our expectancies.

It is therefore quite possible that the varying needs for repetition correspond to varying mental and psychological types. The two great divisions we designate by East and West prove the point without any doubt: East as contemplation, West as action. The music of the East was from its inception, and has remained for centuries up to the present moment, based almost solely on a constant repetition of small structural elements. Western music, originating in Eastern music, may be characterized by a constant striving for new elements of expression.

Whereas no one can foretell with precision how radical the departure from repetition as a basis of music will be in the immediate future, we can speak of a direction: a certain satiety for repetition and an increasing need for newness. The trend is such, and for some of us the idea might be more or less commanding. It would be good to mention in passing that adherence to a strictly nonrepetitional theory would be just as bad as adherence to any other prefixed convention. We might also be aware of the fact that whereas musical works composed on repetitional principles would always stand less and less frequent hearings, compositions avoiding repetitional procedures would be enjoyed more and more on repeated hearings.

But as things stand now, we know that any departure from repetition would result in unconvincing music, wanting in unity and form.

Similarity and contrast, as the two major contradictory factors in the composition of a work of art, have been considered in themselves as good and evil: similarity playing the role of good and contrast the role of evil. Similarity would be the realm of cohesion, unity, organization, and order, and contrast the constant threat of disorder and chaos. Theory and practice have always gone hand in hand in prescribing repetition as the only way to solve the contradiction.

To what extent are we to believe that the great masters

achieved their goal of cohesion and unity by adhering to the established principles of repetition, and not by the strength of their genius?

Indeed, Beethoven took up the tradition he learned from his predecessors and built up that superb marvel of repetitional construction called Symphony No. 5, unsurpassed and unsurpassable, to the point that he himself never tried to repeat his feat in quite the same direction. But is it altogether sacrilegious or nonsensical to think that Beethoven would not have accomplished great things had he not followed the principles of symmetry as closely as he did?

Somehow we cannot help thinking that we owe more to the genius of the man than to the procedures he was historically compelled to follow. No matter what procedures he adopts, the great master is always a great master.

And, indeed, once convinced of that fact, I am not going to deny the infinite possibilities that still may lie in repetition. Let us be neither exclusively in favor of nor thoroughly against any possibility of artistic creation. Let us for that reason explore new directions.

The idea of repetition and variation can be replaced by the notion of constant rebirth, of true derivation: a stream that never comes back to its source; a stream in eternal development, like a spiral, always linked to, and continuing, its original source, but always searching for new and unlimited spaces.

A spiral would perhaps be an answer: an idea that evolves in perpetually renewed forms without ever repeating itself.

The man, his character, what he has to say, his need for communication, all these are in the last analysis the ensemble of deep causes that determine unity and cohesion in a work of art. Unity and cohesion can only be achieved through style.

V

Composer and Public

In past chapters I have referred to the fact that the urge for artistic expression implies a desire to communicate, that is, to establish a dialogue between composer and public. It would be impossible to believe in an extreme position of the ivory tower, where the creative artist, completely isolated, completely self-centered and self-sufficient, would rejoice in the mere fact of creation without any thought of communication with his fellow men. This would only be possible if such a thing as a completely *segregarious* being should exist. But, of course, historically and sociologically, the existence of a truly segregarious individual is impossible; it is merely a theoretical concept. Man is gregarious in every sense: he has need of others just as much as he expects to be needed by others. This is the altruistic part of man, compelling communication and understanding, compelling the desire to share any thoughts or emotions which may be edifying and meaningful. It is in his desire to share the best of his lot that man reveals his better and higher spiritual potentialities.

However, I have mentioned before that a certain amount of incurable loneliness is also present in each one of us. Contradiction seems to be the rule of existence, though very often we do not know how real or fictitious this contradiction may be. Somehow, when a true desire for communication with our fellow men corresponds to our deep, social, gregarious instinct, an inner impulse for sheer monologuing is also present, corresponding, perhaps, to our egoistic, purely individual urge of self-expression.

Dialogue and monologue are the terms of the contradiction: the monologue of a first person speaking to himself, enjoying by himself whatever achievements are the fruit of his own creative abilities, enjoying the mere fact that, in accomplishing the creative act, his pregnancy has ended in a sense of realization and self-satisfaction; and the dialogue of the creative artist—first person—with his public—second person—from which is derived the intense happiness of having something to say and being able to say it in a way convincing and agreeable to others. It is, I do not hesitate to say, a contradiction more apparent than real that all and every artistic creation has such a double intention.

We must not, however, mistake the "monologue" aspect of this double condition of every art creation for the case of an artist who, as is commonly said, is "ahead of his times" and speaks a new and unusual language, very much his own. We say then that he is "misunderstood." How can he communicate with anybody if he speaks a language nobody understands? The masters that have spoken a new and individual language, and departed radically from tradition, have been called revolutionary. The term "revolutionary," by the way, is not so improper after all, if by it we understand a radical or violent change rather than a gradual or evolutionary one. Revolutionary masters have sometimes given the impression of utter individualism and conceit because they do not speak the language everybody understands; they have also given the impression, at times, of insincerity and snobbism, and they have finally been accused of plain ineptitude which, it is said, they try to hide with their innovations or revolutions. We now know that the outstanding revolutionary masters in the history of music were misunderstood just so long as the public did not learn the new language they had invented. But as soon as this happened, the dialogue was established; the public finally caught up with them and ended, sooner or later, by understanding the new language they had not at first comprehended. This is what Ortega y Gasset calls a period of quarantine, which the artist has to endure. At first he may not have an audience, but he is sure he will have one sooner or later, whether he lives to see it or not. It is a simple matter of time.

It is only natural that the creative artist should be ahead of his audience. The creative artist, the composer, is, let us say, a specialist, a technician; he has given all his life to the matter of learning to express himself in music. A creative artist exemplifies intensive education; the audience exemplifies extensive education, extensive both in time and space.

Let us now try to discover whether there is any intention behind the matter of dialogue and monologue. This question of intention will make a lot of difference. Is there ever the intention in creativity to produce pure monologue? Whereas, as I said before, I find it natural and reasonable that in every creation of art there is a good deal of speaking for the sake of speaking, a sort of egoistic pleasure in the process of expression for the sake of expression (which would amount to a desire for monologuing), I am also sure that there is no one who in the last analysis would like to preach in the desert, to speak never to be heard. Every creator hopes, I think, to be eventually heard and understood, after a more or less lengthy quarantine. Everybody would like to make sense to his fellow men: that is natural. An *exclusive* intention of monologuing would be, therefore, almost unthinkable.

Now, on the other hand, would it be possible to envisage an intention of pure dialoguing? Historical fact proves that this has generally been the case. In the past, Haydn and Mozart wrote music at a given salary so that princely audiences would like, understand, and enjoy it. Bach's music was composed with a specific occasion and a specific audience in view. An opera composer, be he Handel or Bellini, wrote music to please his audiences. The same is true in all fields as we go back in the history of music. This is a well-known fact, and yet worth noting. The point I am trying to underline is this: the deliberate purpose of writing for a given audience limits the composer to the taste of that audience, and thus prevents possible discoveries or new and unexpected expressions. When there is a deliberate intention to please the audience the composer carefully thinks of what to say and how to say it in order that his interlocutor may be happy. This implies that the main interest in the creative phenomenon is displaced from the first to the second person; it is the personality of the audience that counts, not that of the creator. This is indeed contrary to our present notion that it is the composer's personality that counts, and it does not make sense that the composer, who is the active, creative party, would be fettered by the passive, static nature of the second, who only listens.

We take for granted that Haydn and Bach and so many others before them were perfectly happy with the situation; they never thought of it in any other terms, or we have not had enough information on the matter. But we know that Mozart hated Salzburg; and we know that when at last he was able to leave, during his final Vienna period, he wrote his most remarkable and individual works; and we know that Beethoven was definitely aware of the fact that it was his audiences who had to conform to his taste and not he to theirs. The nineteenth century inaugurated the era of the "revolutionary" composer, not to mention certain conspicuous cases of innovators in past epochs, such as those around the *Ars Nova* in the fourteenth century. It would seem queer to say that Chopin was very much "misunderstood." His playing was too good and too refined for the common taste of his times, and he was considered a second-class pianist compared with the showy virtuosi of the epoch. It is heartbreaking to remember that he did not dare to play his concertos complete in a public performance; he played separate movements, and between them he smuggled in an array of favorite operatic arias.

Too, it is useless to mention the well-known odysseys of the Berliozes and Wagners, lasting up to the era of the monsters of originality: the fabulous revolutionaries of the late nineteenth and early twentieth centuries, starting with Satie and Debussy. Here is where the traditional, idyllic, peaceful dialogue of past centuries was utterly disrupted: the first person speaking an aggressive, incomprehensible language; the second person, offended, insulted, hissing and cat-calling at the music he is being given as "the music of our times." Is this still a dialogue, in any way?

The fact that the idyllic dialogue was perturbed in such a way has been to the greatest advantage of music. When music was written in accordance with the well-established traditional tastes of the audience, music moved very slowly. As soon as the composer said, *to hell with the public taste, I'll write according to my own taste,* music began to move faster and faster. We are the richer for this apparent maladjustment, and we must be grateful for it.

Somehow, however, contemporary composers seem to be

very much concerned about the situation. In his book *I am a Composer,* Arthur Honegger wrote the following words:

"The career of a musical composer offers the particularity of being the activity and preoccupation of a man that strives to manufacture a product that nobody wants to consume. I would like to compare it to the manufacturer of hats 'Cronstadt,' or high boots with buttons, or corsets 'Mystère.'

"We know in effect how much the public disdains today these objects that yesterday were the sign of the most refined elegance. In music—and it is here where my comparison was false—only things manufactured one hundred years ago are of any value.

"For him [the public] the musical art sums up to the execution of classic and romantic works. The contemporary composer is thus a sort of intruder who absolutely wants to impose himself at a dinner table to which he has not been invited." [1]

Our present-day composers, somewhat upset by this situation, feel like victims of isolation, deprived of a second person to whom to speak; but they fail to realize that our forefathers, the Haydns and the Mozarts, were precisely the victims of their second persons, to whom they had to conform, and please, and speak always in the same conventional, understandable terms. It would be a good, interesting, fictional topic, Johann Sebastian Bach breaking with established rules and becoming an *enfant terrible,* or a revolutionary Haydn besieging the ears of his princely audience.

But is it true that a dialogue is not established between composer and public in our days?

We know that today, as ever before, a composer can be followed by an average audience if he speaks an average language. We know many names in that bracket who enjoy a comfortable dialoguing situation. This remains a traditional position. But the truly modern composer, the one in a progressive (or revolutionary) attitude, finds himself in an awkward position: a composer without a public, to what extent?

"The public." Can we go on speaking of the public as a well-determined value? What do we mean by "public" or by "general public"? Who or what is the public, the modern public? We often hear of sensitive, responsive, intelligent audiences, or the opposite. Also, I have often been questioned on what I think of Latin American audiences compared to North American or European audiences; and someone may mention the "public of Paris" or that of New York. It would be impossible to elucidate this situation if we did not remember that the relation of composer and public is nowadays basically different from what it was in the time of Haydn. In those days the audience was well characterized: it was an audience of the nobility, or of the upper classes, all of very similar tastes and education. It was a special audience. So too were the opera audiences and the Church audiences in those days: homogeneous and special.

Nowadays we are confronted not with special audiences of a homogeneous nature, but with a heterogeneous mass, a very large and diversified mass we call the great public.

The public—the musical public—is an ensemble of persons having a definite interest in music, in which we can recognize two groups: the initiated and the noninitiated. This is perhaps the fundamental difference. In the time of Haydn, only the initiated had any opportunity to hear symphonies: nowadays, everybody has access to music; the noninitiated can hear symphonies, concerts, recordings, radio, and television. The modern public then, is not just large—it is unlimited. While the Esterházy audience was initiated, homogeneous, and limited, ours is partly initiated, partly noninitiated, vastly heterogeneous, and definitely unlimited.

Is this good or bad? To my understanding it is very

good. The noninitiated audience is a potentially initiated
one. There lies the great advantage and unquestionable
progress. While the past conservative audiences were
limited and static, modern audiences are unlimited and
dynamic. They move, they go forward.

Unlimited they are up to a certain extent: that which
we call Western civilization. As unlimited as Western
civilization can be. Oriental or primitive peoples have a
different approach to music: music and the arts in general
remain ritualistic; esthetic considerations are not direct;
traditional canons remain unchanged for centuries, and
so on.

If an Oriental or a primitive man has no initiation in
Western art, he sees or hears nothing, as is the case with
Westerners who are not familiar with Oriental music or
painting. I remember several years ago a group of Pueblo
Indians was brought to a song recital at Carnegie Hall in
New York to hear a program of Schubert and Schumann.
The Indians remained unmoved all the time during the performance. Their hosts were eager at the end to know what
their reaction had been, so they were asked how much they
had enjoyed the music. In a very polite and simple way
they said that the singing had been all right, but they re-
gretted very much that during the performance the singer
had sung the same piece over and over.

It is quite clear that a primitive or an Oriental can be
transculturized, can become a Westerner just as much as a
Westerner can become an Oriental or a primitive if he so
wishes; so that, after all, the great public of our day is
really unlimited even in this respect. This has been proven
by the fact that many Oriental countries such as Japan,
overtaken by Western civilization, now enjoy Bach,
Debussy, or Verdi just as much as any of the Western
countries.

Modern audiences are unlimited and heterogeneous,
which means that really and truly we cannot speak of a

New York or a Paris audience; it means nothing to say that the New York public is progressive or conservative. In New York, as in Paris, or Mexico City, or Buenos Aires, the audiences are a composite of some highly initiated people, some less initiated, some hardly initiated, some very progressive, and some intensely conservative, all with a variety of personal tastes. The only thing we might perhaps be able to say is this: they all begin by liking the romantics and the classics, and gradually learn to enjoy the preclassics and the moderns. I was witness to that evolution in Mexico City, when, in the late twenties, audiences of very limited perspectives violently rejected Debussy and Stravinsky as noisemakers and after twenty years finished by liking them intensely.

So the dialogue is established after all. The progressive artist of today speaks to potential audiences. Since the composer speaks a new language, there can never be ready-made audiences for a given composer. The composer *makes* his audience in the same degree that he *makes* his music; or better, the composer has to have the power to create his music and his music has to have the power to create his audiences. As a result of this vast and fast development of music in the last hundred and fifty years or so, audiences have developed similarly. But audiences per se will always remain—by nature—passive, and the composer will be the active factor who must impress dynamism on potential audiences. It is for this reason that the audience is always posterior to the music: *Pélléas et Mélisande* was first, and in the course of ten or twenty years the audience for *Pélléas et Mélisande* was developed. Static or regressive composers keep the public in stagnation for the same reason that progressive composers develop potential audiences and make them dynamic.

We know of a conspicuous case where the course of musical history has been stopped because composers have been forbidden by state decree to experiment. The State wants the public (they call it the People) to be served and pleased. The State, according perhaps to some estimate, or probably just to a guess, has decreed that the People's taste is equal to n. Therefore, all composers living in the Soviet State have to write music appropriate to the taste equal to n, whether they like it or not.

N taste, or the taste of the People, has been, by the way, rated very low, down to the level of vulgarity, and that is the over-all rule to be followed by composers. It is not, as in the case of Haydn or Bach, that the composer proceeds as he pleases, following what he understands to be music to the best of his knowledge.

If the talent or genius of the composer is crushed, condemned to mediocrity with all its bitter, frustrating implications, the public is disastrously served, for it is deprived of its true and only mentor in the field of the arts—the free creative artist. In fettering and limiting the creative artist, the State condemns the people to eternal mediocrity with no hope for esthetic enrichment. Even if the State were, after a time, to temper its dictates, it would never be able to obtain by bureaucratic procedures what only the genius of a free individual, expressing himself thoroughly and without inhibitions, can obtain.

In the Middle Ages and even later, painters and musicians were very much subject to the rule of the Church: an esthetic rule and an economic subjection. We cannot say that this was an ideal situation—ideal in the sense of liberty of action and unfettered genius—but that was the Middle Ages. The alarming consideration now is that man, having learned so much about freedom in and after the century of the Enlightenment, could return to darkness in the open twentieth century.

It is quite understandable, on the other hand, that a state that is aware of its obligations toward its people should do something about it in matters of art and education, but something creative and intelligent. It is also justifiable to sponsor a certain amount of sheer publicity, as the Church did; publicizing her dogma and sacred history on the walls of convents and churches painted by great masters of the past.

In this connection the Mexican experience of not so many years ago illustrates something essentially different from what has happened in the USSR.

Mexico is a country with a painful, almost tragic history. Three hundred years of colonial domination did not lay the foundation for a well-organized country. At the end of these long, dark centuries, Mexico was in fact a country of slaves, with a small, completely passive middle class. The War of Independence (1810–1821) was not only a revolution for political independence from the crown of Spain, but also a revolution against the prevailing social injustices. The social, political, and economic problems of the newly independent country were big and difficult. Exactly one hundred years after the War of Independence in 1910–1921, a revolution of definitely social character broke out. Ten years of revolution led to the establishment of a stable government under a new and progressive constitution. This was, let us say, "the triumph" of the revolution—though, of course, a triumph can never be achieved; all that can be obtained are more or less small immediate steps forward.

In the year 1921 General Obregón, one of the leaders of the revolution, became President of Mexico. He was a man of a certain vision and wanted to face the important national problems. For the first time in the history of the country a huge budget was allotted to public education, and a man of high caliber, José Vasconcelos, was appointed Secretary. He attacked the basic problems of education, and did not forget to deal with cultural issues on a higher level. A group of painters—among them some of the best, Orozco, Siqueiros, and Rivera—were given the walls of the public buildings for mural painting.

The rebirth of this monumental medium had to be used for monumental purposes. The painters, all claiming to be revolutionaries at heart, decided to paint the revolution. This is important: the painters decided to paint the Revolution, not the State. Vasconcelos, or the government, or the state, never imposed or dictated any theme or subject, let alone any technique, or style, or esthetic. The painters proclaimed that their aim would be to paint for the people. Theirs was a definite desire to establish contact with the people. The problems they faced—the technical problems of clarity (they used to speak of "realism") and style—and the eventual value of their propaganda are not to be considered here. But I must say that when their work had a good, solid artistic value, beyond the avowed purpose of propaganda, it reached important levels that have deserved even international recognition. We used to remark in Mexico: what is the use of revolutionary art if it is not good art? This was not a revolutionary art conforming to any dictate of the State, or any other nonartistic dictate. Each and every artist was free, completely free, to proceed technically and esthetically as he wished.

I do not know whether, in this complete liberty of action, all the artists involved were always one hundred per cent sincere; a considerable amount of demagoguery must have been present. But, on the whole, it is unquestionable that the painters wanted in good faith to use the public walls to gain access to a large audience. It is, I think, also true, and I take it as an important consideration, that in trying to be accessible to the people, as they called it (or, as we would prefer to say, to the average audience), they did not descend to a level of vulgarity. They maintained a classic dignity, at times truly superb, and whether or not they were accessible to the "people," it is good that their work was achieved and stands for posterity.

Not comparable in magnitude or importance, our attempt at a similar program in music took place some years after the Mexican painters had started their movement (1921). When I was appointed Director of the National Conservatory in Mexico, in 1928, I had to face a number of problems of both a technical and social order, which can be met only in a national institution.

Among them was the idea of writing simple, melodic music with a peculiar Mexican flavor that would have a certain dignity and nobility of style; music that would be within the reach of the great mass of people and would eventually take the place of commercial, vulgar music then in great vogue, meant to incite the low passions. This plan included the foundation of choral groups in a rather extended organization and the contributions of composers.

It took some time to accomplish anything. Some choral groups were founded and some music was written, but as the project was beginning to take shape I left the Conservatory (late 1934), and there was nothing anyone could do without the backing of the national institution.

The Mexican experiences are cases in point of so-called "revolutionary purposes." But there are other cases where the creative artist has honestly felt the need for a more direct and immediate relation to his audience—a dialogue without quarantine. I remember the case of composers in the United States who, after having experimented with extremely advanced techniques, tried much more simple and accessible idioms, notably Aaron Copland. In Germany there is the well-known case of Kurt Weill. Whether the American composers had some socio-political idea in mind when they underwent their simplification period I would not be able to say: in a way, that might have been one of the reasons.

But, again, all these were experiments of a certain nature
that composers undertook of their own free will, and each
possessed and followed his own views in his own way, with
no political or technical dictates from the State or any other
agency. There was nothing but the spontaneous—free and
unforced—desire of each composer to approach a problem
of vital interest to him. Their freedom was such that they
proceeded with their experiment just as long as they
wished; and it remained spontaneous, also, in that whatever inducements they had, they wanted to try out possible solutions by themselves. In the case of the Mexican
painters there was a definite socio-political motive related
to the revolutionary exaltation. In the case of composers of
other countries a similar motivation might have been observed; in the nineteen-thirties a rather general tendency
existed, among artists and intellectuals, toward a more conscious attitude about social problems.

Probably, however, this was not the only consideration.
Composers were not entirely happy writing music for present small, or hypothetically large future, audiences. They
probably felt isolated within the four walls of a thoroughly
outdated ivory tower. They would have preferred to feel
more useful to their community, and perhaps also to attain
all that comes with it in greater or lesser degree: prestige,
money, or both. One remembers the case of Mozart, often
referred to in those days as a major composer who wrote
for immediate consumption and yet became in after centuries one of the "immortals."

We may consider as one more reason for these experiments the growing taste for simplification as such, preva-
lent in those years, together with a taste for folk, native
music; the two blended very handily. All these efforts
toward a greater dialogue element have been good experiments and experiences, and can teach us very valuable
lessons.

To conclude: when works of art are created in view of a given audience, stagnation is inevitable. Putting it in very direct terms, composer and public are not on the same level. The composer should always remain uppermost. If the composer wants to get to the audience's level, he will have to descend, and he can never do so without risking all possibility of moving forward. A great composer is one who has many things to teach others, things that were not known before. The audience, the second person, can never speak in equal terms with the composer, for the creator always knows more. Thus, there is a great deal of monologue for a composer who keeps in his place. He should be prepared for that, and for the inevitable quarantine. The over-all consideration for a composer in this matter should be that, if he does not succeed sooner or later in creating an audience, it is, in the last analysis, due to the inability of his work to achieve such a definite and ultimate purpose.

Now, I cannot really finish the matter of the relationship between composer and public without considering the special circumstances determined by the presence of an intermediary person: the interpreter, or performer.

To what extent does the audience receive a genuine image of the composer's conception through the performer's "interpretation"?

A few quotations from Beethoven's letters provide us with valuable examples. Carl Czerny related the following:

"When I played the quintet with wind instruments at Schuppanzigh's concert, I allowed myself in my youthful frivolity, many changes—increasing the difficulty of passages, using the higher octaves, etc. Beethoven very properly and severely upbraided me for it, in the presence of Schuppanzigh, Linke and the other players. The next day I received from him the following letter, which I copy exactly from the original lying before me:

'I cannot see you today, tomorrow I will come to you in person to talk with you. I burst out so yesterday, I was very sorry after it had happened, but you must pardon it in an author who would have preferred to hear his work just as he wrote it . . .'"[2]

There seems to be a general idea that, whereas nobody would dare to change a chord or note in the recognized masterpieces of the great composers, it is quite permissible to change freely any tempi, dynamics, or expression marks: and the feeling goes even further in considering it good and desirable that the performer do so as a way of projecting "his" interpretation.

This is a point of extreme importance, and I would like to emphasize the fact that whereas the change of a note here and there damages the musical work in particular given spots, the alteration of tempi and dynamics produces an over-all deformation, a complete upheaval in the conception, form, meaning, and expression of the whole work.

Another letter of Beethoven on this matter is written to the opera singer Friedir Sebastian Mayer, concerning the revival of *Fidelio,* now in two acts, March and April 1806.

Please request Herr v. Seyfried to conduct my opera today; I myself want today to see and hear it at a distance; by that means, at any rate, my patience will not be so severely tried, as when close by I hear my music murdered. I cannot help thinking that it is done purposely. I say nothing about the wind instruments, but all *pp, crescendos,* all *decrescendos,* and all *fortes ff* were struck out of my opera; no notice is taken of a single one. If that's what I have to hear, there is no inducement to write anything more! . . .

Your friend,

BEETHOVEN.[3]

His superb attention to detail, with all kinds of signs to indicate dynamics, tempi, and attacks, is obvious in all of his scores, but his remarks in writing on the subject of precision to his copyists are really worth noting. The following is a letter to Carl Holz written in 1825:

Best *violino secundo*

Read *Violino 2do!* The passage in the first *Allegro* in the 1st violin, so

play it thus; also in the first Allegro just follow these marks of *expression* in the four parts:

The notes are all right—only understand me rightly.

Now about your copy, my good friend. *Obligatissimo—ma,* the signs p $<$ $>$ &c., are terribly neglected, and often, very often, in the wrong place—no doubt owing to hurry. For heaven's sake please impress on Rampel to write everything as it stands; now only look carefully at what I have corrected, and you will find all that you have to say to him; where · is over the note, there must be no ♪ also vice versa!

♪ ♪ ♪ and ♪ ♪ ♪ are not the same thing. The $<$ are often inten-

tionally placed after the notes, for instance,  The slurs

just as they now stand! It is not a matter of indifference whether

you play ⌒ or ⌒ !

Mind, this comes from a high quarter. I have spent no less than the whole morning and the whole of yesterday afternoon with the correction of the two pieces, and am quite hoarse with swearing and stamping.

> In great haste, yours
>
> BEETHOVEN.[4]

His preoccupation with the accuracy of tempi was out-standing. He was really the first great musician to realize the meaning of tempo as a fundamental element of the musical creation. The following letter speaks by itself on his enthusiasm over a way to remedy forever the imperfect indication of tempi by means of Italian words.

To the Aulic Councillor v. Mosel   (1817?)

I heartily rejoice in the same opinion, which you share with me in regard to the terms indicating time-measure which have been handed down to us from the barbarous period of music. For, only to name one thing, what can be more senseless than *allegro* which, once for all, means *merry,* and how far off are we frequently from such conception of this time-measure, in that the music itself expresses something quite contrary to the term. So far as the four principal movements are concerned, but which are far from having the truth or importance of the four principal winds, we consider them last. It is another matter with words indicating the character of a piece; these we cannot give up, as time refers rather to the body, whereas *these are already themselves related to the soul of the piece.* As for me, I have often thought of giving up these senseless terms, Allegro, Andante, Adagio, Presto, and for this Maelzel's metronome offers the best opportunity. I herewith give you *my word,* that I will *no more* use them in my new compositions. It is another question whether by this means we shall bring the M[etronome] into the so necessary *general* use. I scarcely think so. I have no doubt they will call out that I am a *despot;* anyhow, that would be better than to accuse us of *feudalism.* Hence I am of opinion that the best thing for our country, when once *music* has become a National Want, and every village schoolmaster would have to promote the use of the Metr., would be for Maelzel to seek to bring out by subscription a certain number of metronomes at a higher price; and when the number covers his expenses, he will be able to supply the other necessary Metron. for the Musical National Want, and at so cheap a rate, that we may expect them to become in general and widespread use. It is, of course, understood that some persons must place themselves at the head of such a movement to give a stimulus to it; so far as I am of any influence you may certainly count on me, and with pleasure I await the post which you will herein assign to me.

Sir,

With high esteem,
Yours most devotedly,
LUDWIG VAN BEETHOVEN.[5]

"The terms indicating time-measure which have been handed down to us from the barbarous period of music," implies quite a violent protest against anarchy in tempo markings, such as were in use before Beethoven. And ten years later, a few months before his death, in December 1826, he said in a letter to B. Schott and Sons in Mainz: "The metronome marks will shortly follow: do wait for them. In our age such things are certainly necessary; also I hear from Berlin that the first performance of the Symphony [he means the Ninth] went off with enthusiasm, which I ascribe in great part to the metronome marking. We can scarcely have any more *tempi ordinari,* for one must follow the ideas of unfettered genius." [6]

In the last paragraph of what seems to be the last letter Beethoven ever wrote, he shows his obsession over the matter of correct tempi to be very much alive. Moscheles was to do the Ninth Symphony in London and Beethoven wanted to send him, personally, the metronomic indications. The following is the last paragraph of a letter written to Moscheles on 18 March 1827 (eight days before his death): "Your noble behaviour I shall never forget, and I shall soon render my thanks in particular to Sir Smart and Herr Stumpf. The metronomised Ninth Symphony please hand to the Philarmonic Society. Enclosed find the markings." [7]

What all this seems to mean is that the man wanted two main things to happen: his musical conceptions to be accurately fixed by notation, and the performer to follow and obey his indications. He wanted the "barbarous period of music" to come to an end.

The "barbarous period" was that in which the virtuosi, which he detested, used music for purposes of showmanship; or, simply, that long historical period, which Beethoven definitely brought to an end, when the composer's conception was not finished in his own mind and he therefore wrote it down incompletely and imperfectly, leaving a great deal to the interpreter's initiative—who was, then, a

true interpreter, in the sense that he had to elucidate un-
clear or unfinished texts.

It is obvious that notation grew more and more perfect
as the composer's ideas grew clearer and clearer. Boileau
in his work *L'Art poétique* says:

> Avant donc que d'écrire apprenez à penser.
> Selon que notre idée est plus ou moins obscure,
> L'expression la suit, ou moins nette, ou plus pure:
> Ce que l'on conçoit bien s'énonce clairement. . . .[8]

> "That which is well conceived is clearly expressed."

In fact, for centuries before Beethoven music was not
clearly expressed because it was not well conceived, that
is, thoroughly conceived. Beethoven was the first to conceive it well and thoroughly, and so to express it.

In the present state of affairs there seems to be a serious
discussion on how much liberty the performer should have.
But nothing can end this discussion because the performer
is free to do what he wants.

It is perhaps not clear to many people that in a work of
art there are no insignificant or unimportant things; there
are neither basic elements nor unessential details. Everything pertaining to a masterpiece is equally significant and
important. Can we say that the colors, the shade of colors,
the forms, the balance of forms, the composition, that any of
these elements is more or less important than the others in
a Cézanne canvas? The same is true in music, to exactly the
same degree, in form, harmony, tone color, balance of
sound, tempi, variations of tempi, shades of sound color, and
so on.

In reality, in the case of painting and sculpture the artist's
conception fulfills itself in a material object: a canvas or a
sculpture. Any one is free to retouch or change or remodel
a masterpiece of painting or sculpture, but nobody would
dare or want to do such a thing. Why, then, do it in music?

The composer's conception fulfills itself in a paper with musical signs. Notation, with all its limitations, is very objective and quite satisfactory. The problem is not so much the matter of notation as it is the attitude of performers or so-called interpreters.

We composers want our ideas thoroughly expressed in notation and genuinely translated by the performer. But performers, however clear the musical notation may be, are not always willing to reflect the text in its purity; they want to add something of themselves, and there has not as yet been established a court of appeals for composers.

No matter how much current interpretations may depart from the letter of the conception, the original work remains intact in its original purity. But although theoretically nothing can change the original conception, it is a fact that audiences are gradually getting used to interpretations that diverge widely from the original: we all have witnessed in the last twenty-five years a Debussy that loses conciseness and subtlety and a Stravinsky that loses precision and crispness in the hands of their interpreters. This is something of which we are sure. Of a Chopin losing sensitiveness, poetry, and finesse to gain a species of thick sentimentalism, we can only guess; of a Beethoven losing drama to gain overdramatization we also can only guess. If I mention this, it is not only to put in a completely useless complaint against a good many current interpreters, but to suggest the possibility of a new trend in the performer's attitude, an attitude that would enable him to approach his task, and use all his talent and interpreting abilities, with the definite aim of discovering the true, complete, and inner intentions of the composer. After all, who knows more about Beethoven's intentions, and Beethoven's music, than Beethoven himself?

This, then, would be the interpreter who, instead of

molding the musical work to his technical abilities and esthetic leanings, would mold his esthetic leanings and technical abilities to serve the composer's conception.

In fact, the true interpretation of a piece of music is that which does not alter the text, and succeeds in giving a living pulse to it in its re-creation. Departing from the texts, thousands of interpretations of Beethoven might please millions of listeners; but we are not certain of what Beethoven himself would think, or if he would not repeat: "If that's what I have to hear, there is no inducement to write anything more!"

We do not have to alter the work of art itself to change our approach to it, as is clear in the case of the plastic arts. It has not occurred to anybody to say that in order to like a Da Vinci painting we should have to make alterations in it. In the same way the musical work does not have to be altered. It is we who alter and change in the presence of a work of art, in infinite ways and moods and in approaches to its message. We constantly discover new aspects and expressions in it.

A work of art does not change; it should not be changed. In common life we are accustomed to think with reason that anything and everything is perfectible. But the masterpiece of art is the exception: it is the impeccably finished product—there is nothing to be added, nothing to be taken away from it. It is there forever, in its imperturbable, undaunted perfection.

VI

The Enjoyment of Music

The enjoyment of music, and, in general, the enjoyment of art, is one of those special prerogatives for which one can never be grateful enough.

The delectation in art expression is perhaps among the highest attributes of the human spirit. That attribute is given in varying degrees to human beings, but very likely it is not denied to anybody, no matter in how small a degree; and, surely, there is always the latent possibility of increasing it.

It is wonderful to realize that we live in an era where the benefits of education are not confined to exclusive minorities. Education is taken care of by the State, and is done on a national scale, but other agents of public education besides the State are innumerable and of infinite power. I am not going to discuss them here, of course, as I just want to

107

detach certain facts: educators have enhanced the importance of art in any program of public education, which
means that music and art are cultivated in schools, colleges,
and universities; and art and musical institutions are spon-
sored by both the State and private enterprises. Furthermore, the remarkable and rapid advancements in science
have provided means of recording and communication,
such as the phonograph, radio, movies, and television, that
contribute very efficient material aid to the purposes of
education.

I should like to mention in passing that it is impossible
to say that such mechanical means have been used fully for
the benefit of truly educational purposes; in many cases,
such vehicles have been used to lower the public taste rather
than to raise and cultivate it. This would be a subject for
a chapter in itself. But no one can deny the possibilities involved, nor the fact that whatever little has been done in
a good direction has been of tremendous help to the cause
of musical education.

Of course, we can speak of musical education for professionals and of musical education for the general mass of
public. It is quite clear that the man or woman who decides
to embrace the musical profession is a person that has a
natural liking for music; that is, he enjoys music in a spontaneous and more or less intense manner. This would be a
person born musical, the possessor of a natural musical
sense, for whom music is the fundamental if not the only
thing in life. The person that is studying to become a professional is doing so because he enjoys music and wants to
derive such satisfaction from it. The whole premise of his
or her decision to become a professional is the love and enjoyment of music.

In the past, musical education was for a long time confined to the professional. Nowadays we have another kind
of musical education for all those who are not professionals,

for the overwhelming majority. They are not bound to learn
the deep secrets of the trade. They are bound, simply, to
learn to enjoy music.

To enjoy music, as a pure, abstract thing, is a matter of
much more consequence than it appears at first sight. The
enjoyment of music comes from our esthetic sense, or artistic talent, and much has been said about it. German philosophers in the last century proclaimed a theory very much
in favor: that an overflow of vital energies, idleness and
play, make art possible. They claimed art disposes of superfluous energies in the one who creates it. In inferior animals
—they went on—all vital energy is used up to secure the life
of the individual and the species. Man, however, having
overcome that stage, disposes of a superabundance of energy, usable for play and art. But, indeed, not only superabundance of energy can make art: esthetic intuition is also
needed.

To us, now, it is quite clear that idleness is the basic element in artistic creation, but in quite a different way. One
has to be free of "occupations" to be able to occupy oneself
with something. I would like to emphasize the fact that the
composer's job is a full-time job. Indeed, one has to be idle
—free of any other occupation—in order to give to composition whatever energies and superabundance of energies
one may have. In the same sense, a banker or any other
practitioner has also to be idle, in order to attend fully to
his business. Idleness in that sense, yes: but not in the sense
of a luxury born of a surplus of energies, or in the sense
that the creation of art is a sort of pastime, mixed in with
idleness and play.

As a matter of fact, all great composers have been men
of tremendous strength and have put all of it into their task
of composition. Even those considered somewhat fragile,
such as Chopin or Mozart, worked heavily by any stand-
ards: only think of the amount of time and energy needed

to put down in writing the thousands of manuscript pages they wrote in their lifetime!

The theory that acknowledges a dynamic, innate force in all sorts of ideas, helps to explain clearly the tremendous strength that men of ideas can develop. According to that theory, every thought or idea is an incipient action. Every spiritual intention tends to movement and action. Ideas, in themselves, contain the life germ of their own active realization.

The artistic idea, therefore, has in itself the elements impelling it to find expression. So ideas are themselves live beings, moving and acting, looking for their way out and for whatever they may need to achieve their end.

Musical ideas, coming from the inner self of the composer, have to struggle with whatever limitations and contradictions there may be in the exterior, this being another factor in their ultimate development, and, I may say, no mean factor. I mention it as one more instance of the tremendous amount of energies the creative man has to put into his work.

Freud says that artistic talent is still a "psychological enigma." We are not interested in deciphering such an enigma: we are simply interested in the fact of the existence of artistic talent. According to him we, so-called civilized men, under the pressure of our repressions, do not find reality entirely satisfactory; and we then lead a life of phantasy, to compensate for what is missing in actual reality. The man, unadjusted to reality, who possesses artistic talent can transform his phantasies into artistic creations.

Whether or not phantasies, or phantasy, are a compensation for maladjustment is not to be discussed here either, but there can be no question that phantasy and artistic talent are the indispensable elements of creation.

Wilhelm Worringer says: "By 'absolute artistic volition' is to be understood that latent inner demand which exists *per se,* entirely independent of the object and of the mode of creation, and behaves as will to form. It is the primary factor in all artistic creation and, in its innermost essence, every work of art is simply an objectification of this *a priori* existent absolute artistic volition."[1]

Most of these theories have been developed in view of the phenomenon of artistic creation. To what extent do they apply also to the phenomenon of artistic contemplation?

The man who looks at a canvas or listens to music is passive, but he is passive only to the extent that he is unable to create. For in listening to the music he is active; he is going through the same needs of expression, and the same self-projection, that the creator went through. It has been repeatedly said that the listener likes the music in which he finds himself, in which he recognizes his own emotions and tastes.

But it all comes from the same point: artistic talent. It is all a matter of degree. Whereas the creator possesses this in superlative degree, so that his ideas have the implicit dynamism to convert themselves into works of art, the listener's initiative moves him not to create, but to look for creations already made.

In fact, when a person listens to a piece of music, he is going through the same mental, emotional, psychological, and intellectual processes that the composer went through. The listener, the true listener, is not passive; he is active, listens actively, and can listen more or less actively. (We would not, of course, consider the man who hears without listening.)

' To listen more and more actively, more and more intensely, more and more intelligently, more and more comprehensibly, is a matter of education. To this end, there have been, in recent years, very encouraging signs.

Even in less recent times we can find evidence of such educational trends in the writings of the great masters

themselves. Schumann, Liszt, and Wagner were superb at
explaining their own ideas and purposes and esthetic con-
victions to the public. They were in fact great musical
pedagogues. Debussy taught essential lessons in his critical
writings, some of which were later on selected and published
under the title *M. Croche Anti-dilettante*. Stravinsky and
Copland are also wonderfully articulate teachers in their
numerous writings, not to mention the great composers who
have written purely didactic works, such as Berlioz, Hinde-
mith, Schoenberg, and Piston. There seems to be a very
definite desire in great composers to explain themselves to
others, to justify their beliefs, to gain proselytes for their
music and their ideas. And besides having the authority,
they are good writers. The result is that all of this has been
convincing and of enormous educational value both to
musicians and audiences.

But the development of recent years that I mentioned
before is something else: it is that specialized branch of education called "music appreciation," directed expressly to the
development of more intelligent or appreciative audiences.

How could the aims of music appreciation be described?
I think they are, ideally, the development of the innate
musical sense of a person, and the provision of increasing
technical means to understand the achievements of a work.
Busoni speaks of the public in Germany as being ideal in
the sense that every person not only is "very fond of music,"
but understands it "as regards its technical means of expression," and this is to him a "musical" person.

"A musical person," he says, "is one who manifests an
inclination for music by a nice discrimination and sensitiveness with regard to the *technical aspects* of the art. By
'technics' I mean rhythm, harmony, intonation, part-leading, and the treatment of themes. The more subtleties he is
capable of hearing or reproducing in these, the more 'musical' he is held to be." [2]

And this is precisely what the texts on musical appreciation do: they introduce the auditor to the technical realm
of music in a way that is accessible and interesting. Rhythm,
harmony, intonation, part-leading, and the treatment of
themes should not be mysteries to anybody. All these are
simple things to grasp and comprehend and, once one is
initiated, add enormously to the enjoyment of music. To
be thus initiated is the starting point of an endless road to
a greater and more profound understanding of music.

To this end we have seen the publication in recent years
of innumerable articles and books; special courses in schools,
colleges, and universities, and on the radio; and an outstanding experiment, a remarkable confabulation of choice ingredients—television, the New York Philharmonic Symphony
Orchestra, and its musical director, the composer-conductor
Leonard Bernstein. A notable pedagogue, he has caught the
interest of millions, evoking or provoking their taste for the
sheer beauty of music by various means, one of them providing convincing and simple explanations of its technical
make-up. This experiment is a transcendental departure
from custom; it is for the good of the enjoyment of music;
that is, for the good of the millions of people who will discover and increase their capacity to enjoy music.

The artistic education of the masses on a large scale poses
certain problems. We are used to thinking of the masses as
intrinsically inferior, in opposition to select, cultivated minorities, with the natural consequence that we always think
of select art for the minority and inferior art for the masses.

Of course, I am not going to enter into generalizations but
certain facts speak eloquently for themselves. As I have
said in a previous chapter, the great public—or the mass
public—cannot be looked at as a solid block of homogeneous
tastes and cultural levels. And it is also certain that the
eternal progress of music and its increasing circulation mean
that the mass public, no matter how "mass" and how great,

is dynamic: it moves, it progresses. In my childhood Mozart and Beethoven were still only for the minorities; in my youth, Debussy was for the select few. In less than a lifetime Debussy has almost reached the mass public, let alone Mozart and Beethoven; as we come to this conclusion, we approach the subject of the final judgment. No matter how pejorative our attitude about the great mass, it is the great public, the great mass, that eventually does pronounce the final judgment. It is inconceivable that Mozart, Beethoven, Chopin, Wagner, and Debussy would have remained forever composers for minorities—just as fifty years ago it was inconceivable that the grocery man, the butcher, and the barber would enjoy the Fifth or the Seventh Symphony of Beethoven. And they do now. No matter how snobbish we really love to be, and how esoteric, we shall have to admit as an incontestable fact that the approval of the great public constitutes the supreme pronouncement or the touchstone of the greatness of a composer. As a matter of fact, we call a great composer the man who in the course of time has been consecrated by the great public.

To what degree are the minorities more rigid, less dynamic, than the great masses? This would be an interesting subject, but somewhat difficult to clarify. In other words: is the avant-garde of forty years ago apt to be the avant-garde of today? Would those who have enjoyed Debussy ever since the premier of *Pélléas* in 1902 be able to enjoy Schoenberg and Webern twenty-five years later? The question seems rather complex, but somehow my answer would be that, although we may be sure that the great public is always right in the long run, we cannot be equally sure that the minorities are always right in the short run. How many minorities of the last forty years—no matter how small and how noisy—have completely disappeared from our recollection, together with their worshipped heroes!

In fact, we cannot be sure that minorities will always be right, because they lack perspective. In art, the judicial power cannot be exercised without perspective, perspective in time.

There are minorities at all times. There are minorities now; and we are not always sure of the aptitude and the sincerity of new experiments. Because, of course, it is new and experimental truths that minorities look for.

I have said previously that a masterpiece is always an experiment, an experiment that proved to be successful, and the proof can only be discerned in the course of time.

There are means of only very limited or relative value to judge a new experiment. I would venture to say that possibilities of success could only be grounded on the degree of sincerity with which it is carried out. A great deal of theorizing always accompanies a new departure. Think of the amount of time—almost two centuries—during which have appeared equal temperament, and Bach's preference for the major and minor scales over the modal; the infinite Wagnerian theories, and the many theoretical propositions of Satie, Debussy, and Stravinsky; more recently, the theories on atonality, and composition with twelve-note series; and still more recently, *musique concrète* and electronic music.

There has always been a great deal of theorizing about new trends in music, and one can never know at the outset how good the new theories are; given that the theories are good, one can never know how much the composer is the master or the victim of his theories. It is really a twofold problem: the theories must be good and must be applied to good advantage.

However, presupposing even the most correct and solid theories, there will always be reservations. Very often theories end by converting themselves into what are called "techniques," as we, for instance, speak of "twelve-tone technique." Whether this is a technique or a given procedure in composition, the fact remains that it comes from preconceived theories on how music should be integrated (or organized) in order to achieve cohesion, unity, and style; that is to say, in order to achieve beauty. It is unquestionable that beauty, already created and accepted as such, can be subjected to detailed and intelligent analysis, and certain general principles established as to how and why that beauty was achieved. In that way we derive theoretical principles from created beauty. But can we derive beauty from theoretical principles?

There is no doubt that certain given procedures can lead to very attractive results; it is true that the most remarkable and unexpected music can come out of pre-established compositional devices manipulated with ingenuity. But it is my belief that if anything of real beauty comes out, it is not due to the compositional procedures so ingeniously manipulated, but to something more, which cannot be codified, which comes from the specifically musical genius of the composer.

I have often been asked what should be the position of a Latin American composer vis-à-vis dodecaphony. I do not think the position of a Latin American composer should be any different from that of any other composer of any other land. A composer should know everything that has been done in composition before him: know it well and thoroughly. But he should not follow any rules in writing his music, because in music there are no general rules; there are only special rules, personal rules: Wagner's rules were good for Wagner, and Schoenberg's for Schoenberg. A composer should not stick to a given school, but should profit from all schools. It has been said with reason that "the function of a creative artist consists in making laws, not in following laws ready made." [3]

But the idea of "making laws" should not be taken literally. It does not mean that the creative artist should first make certain laws and then make music according to them. Music should never come from the conscious application of laws, rules, or "techniques," but has to be first heard in the head; from there it should be transposed to the paper. In fact, laws should be made *ex post facto* and applied subconsciously.

The emphasis given in our day—and also in past epochs—to pre-established organizational principles has had a curious result: the composer thinks of the plan of his composition, and of the principles according to which every phase of it is to be organized, but he knows or thinks nothing or very little of the music that will result. If he writes according to that plan, some music has to come out; and if the plan is good and the principles correctly manipulated, the music that comes out has to be good, too; and very often it is—in a fashion. Anything can be good without being totally good. I think it is essential that music be originated in the composer's inner self, and that every inch of its creation be the result of a specifically musical thought and sensitivity, from a musical mind, a musical imagination, a musical phantasy, and the *a priori* artistic volition of which the work of art is an objectification.

The process of creating a work of art is the act of discharging a musical charge. Musical images, phantasies, and hallucinations make a musical charge, and the composer's second task is to give expression to the music he has actually heard within himself.

Somehow the pre-eminence of prefabricated techniques has led composers to write down notes on paper, whereas the composer should have to write down the sounds in his heart.

One often hears people speaking of sincerity in creation. I have spoken of sincerity as perhaps the only ingredient vital to the success of new artistic experiments in the future. But what is sincerity; what do we mean by that? I do not know: but I would say that there is sincerity when there is joy in musical creation, when there is true musical enjoyment in it. To create is to give birth. There is joy in giving birth; pain overcome by joy! There are many things that can be simulated. True enjoyment cannot.

Worringer has referred to beauty in very simple terms: "The value of a work of art, what we call its beauty, lies, generally speaking, in its power to bestow happiness." [4]

Yes, joy and happiness of a certain nature: for we can be mistakenly joyful and happy, as we often mistake evil for good. Mistaken and ephemeral happiness can lead to debasement and degeneration. But the miracle of art consists in providing the kind of enjoyment and happiness that nothing renders low, and it all and permanently elevates and edifies.

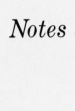

Notes

NOTES

Chapter I. A Latin American Composer

1. Jules Combarieu, *La Musique, ses lois, son évolution* (Paris: Ernest Flammarion, Editeur, 1907).

2. Jules Combarieu, *La Musique et la magie* (Paris: Alphonse Picard et Fils, Editeurs, 1909), p. 243.

3. José Ortega y Gasset, *La Deshumanización del arte,* Obras Completas, Tomo III (Madrid: Revista de Occidente, 1925).

4. See Antonello Gerbi, *La Disputa del Nuovo Mondo, storia di una polemica* (Milano: Riccardo Ricciardi Editore, 1955).

5. Alfonso Reyes, "The Position of America," in *The Position of America and Other Essays,* tr. Harriet de Onís (New York: Alfred Knopf, 1950).

6. Louis Moreau Gottschalk (1829–1869), Louisiana-born French Creole, whose tremendous success as a pianist and composer was due as much to his showmanship as his virtuosity.

7. See Alejo Carpentier, *La Música en Cuba* (México: Fondo de Cultura Económica, 1945).

Chapter II. Art as Communication

1. Charles Darwin, *The Descent of Man* (New York: Modern Library edition).

2. Darwin, *Descent of Man.*

3. Igor Stravinsky, *Poetics of Music,* tr. Arthur Knodel and Ingolf Dahl (Cambridge: Harvard University Press, 1947), pp. 70–71.

4. Victor Hugo, *William Shakespeare* (Paris: J. Hetzel et Cie., A. Quantin, 1882).

5. Arnold Hauser, *The Social History of Art,* tr. S. Godman, with the author (New York: Alfred A. Knopf, 1952).

6. Everard M. Upjohn, Paul S. Wingert, Jane Gaston Mahler, *History of World Art,* 2nd ed. (New York: Oxford University Press, 1958).

7. Gianbattista Vico, *The New Science,* tr. from the third edition (1744) by Thomas Goddard Bergin and Max Harold Fisch (Ithaca: Cornell University Press, 1948).

8. Vico, *New Science.*

Chapter III. Form in Music

1. *The New York Times,* November 28, 1959.

2. James Frazer, *The Golden Bough* (New York: St. Martin's Press, 1955).

3. Combarieu, *La Musique et la magie.*

4. Frances Densmore, *Papago Music,* Bulletin 90, Smithsonian Institution, Bureau of American Ethnology (Washington: Government Printing Office, 1929).

5. Aristotle, *Art of Poetry,* tr. W. Hamilton Fyfe (Oxford: Clarendon Press, 1952).

6. Aristotle, *Politica,* ed. Benjamin Jowett (Oxford: Clarendon Press, 1921).

7. The denomination *spondee-anapest* according to Combarieu, *Histoire de la musique,* I (Paris: Librairie Armand Colin, 1913).

8. "Time," in *Grove's Dictionary of Music and Musicians* (New York: St. Martin's Press, Inc., 1955).

9. Combarieu, *La Musique et la magie.*

10. See Franz Boas, *General Anthropology* (Boston: D. C. Heath and Company, 1938).

11. André Breton, *Manifest du surréalism* (Paris: Editions Kra, 1929).

12. Aristotle, *Art of Poetry.*

13. Aristotle, *Art of Poetry.*

14. Aristotle, *Art of Poetry.*

Chapter IV. Repetition in Music

1. Lincoln Kirstein, "What Ballet is About: An American Glossary," *Dance Perspectives,* No. 1, Winter 1959 (Brooklyn, N. Y.).

Chapter V. Composer and Public

1. Arthur Honegger, *Je suis compositeur* (Paris: Edition du Conquistador, 1951).

2. Alexander Wheelock Thayer, *The Life of Ludwig van Beethoven*, ed. and rev. Henry E. Krehbiel (New York: The Beethoven Association, 1921).

3. *Beethoven's Letters*, tr. J. S. Shedlock (London: J. M. Dent and Co., 1909).

4. *Beethoven's Letters.*

5. *Ibid.*

6. *Ibid.*

7. *Ibid.*

8. Boileau-Despréaux, *L'Art poétique* (Leipzig: Libraire de E. Wengler, Editeur, 1856).

Chapter VI. The Enjoyment of Music

1. Wilhelm Worringer, *Abstraction and Empathy: A Contribution to the Psychology of Style,* tr. Michael Bullock (New York: International Universities Press, Inc., 1953).

2. Ferruccio Busoni, *Sketch of a New Esthetic of Music* (New York: G. Schirmer, 1911).

3. Busoni, *Sketch.*

4. Worringer, *Abstraction and Empathy.*

Index